MW01241017

Advance comments on *The Art of Coping* . . .

"*The Art of Coping* is an extraordinarily relevant, practical, and moving document. In the face of adversity and tragedy, it can help us remember where our supports lie. It is eminently readable, drawing from diverse sources. Its organization will be helpful both to those in need and professional caregivers."

—Robert M. Magrisso, M.D.
General Internist, Evanston Hospital,
Northwestern University Medical School

"Written from deep experience and compassion, *The Art of Coping* is straightforward and full of common sense. It will surely be helpful to many."

—Gunilia Norris, author of
Being Home and *Journeying in Place*

"Dr. Halligan's book holds a unique place in the wide spectrum of works on the topic. It emphasizes a holistic rather than reductionistic perspective and successfully blends behavioral science and spirituality approaches. Rich with clinical vignettes and wisdom, her book offers the reader a soothing balm for the sometimes unforeseen and painful vicissitudes of life. It gently leads one to greater self-knowledge and has much to offer both health professionals and the greater public."

—Frederick W. Foley, Ph.D., Training Director
Graduate Psychology, Yeshiva University
Albert Einstein College of Medicine

"Dr. Halligan provides a practical, readable tool for those searching for better ways of coping with life's challenges. Its blending of Eastern and Western thinking and rich clinical examples will appeal to professionals, both to enhance their own understanding and as a source for bibliotherapy for their patients. Her writing demonstrates her thoughtfulness and sensitivity to the anxieties within us all."

—Steven Rothke, Ph.D., Chief of Psychology
Rehabilitation Institute of Chicago

The Art of
COPING

The Art of
COPING

— ❖ —

Fredrica R. Halligan, Ph.D.

CROSSROAD • NEW YORK

1995

The Crossroad Publishing Company
370 Lexington Avenue, New York, NY 10017

Copyright © 1995 by Fredrica R. Halligan

Printed in the United States of America

Library of Congress Cataloging-in-Publication Data

Halligan, Fredrica R.
    The art of coping / Fredrica R. Halligan.
        p.   cm.
    Includes bibliographical references.
    ISBN: 0-8245-1487-4 (pbk.)
    1. Adjustment (Psychology) 2. Adjustment (Psychology)—Case
studies. 3. Stress management. I. Title.
BF335.H25 1995
155.9'042—dc20   95-3882
                                                              CIP

To my children and my patients,
all those who have taught me
so much

Contents

———— ❖ ————

Acknowledgments

❖

I AM ESPECIALLY GRATEFUL to those who have inspired, encouraged and mentored this work: Marvin Reznikoff and Georgiana Shick Tryon at Fordham University, the late R. Tomas Agosin at Albert Einstein College of Medicine, and Murray Stein at the C. G. Jung Institute of Chicago. Those friends who have helped me to edit and consolidate vast quantities of anecdotes into a coherent manuscript have my unending appreciation: Richard Grossman, John Shea, Ewert Cousins, and Michael Halligan. I owe gratitude to my own support network, including Silvia Perera, Thayer Green, and Bob Tolz, and especially to faithful friends, Ben and Elaine Brady, Betty and Jim Ebzery, Jim and Sue Nash, who have always modeled sane coping; we have shared rich dialog out of which this book has emerged. Finally, for the mechanics of production, I am deeply grateful to Mary Conetta, who has adapted remarkably in order to type and refine so many pages during all the stages of this book's growth, and to Michael Leach at Crossroad, who had the vision to discover a publishable manuscript and carry it through to completion.

Introduction

The Varieties of Coping Experience

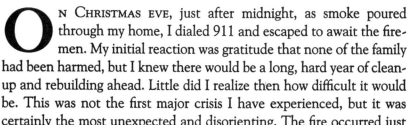

O N CHRISTMAS EVE, just after midnight, as smoke poured through my home, I dialed 911 and escaped to await the firemen. My initial reaction was gratitude that none of the family had been harmed, but I knew there would be a long, hard year of cleanup and rebuilding ahead. Little did I realize then how difficult it would be. This was not the first major crisis I have experienced, but it was certainly the most unexpected and disorienting. The fire occurred just when I was completing the major revisions of this book. As I moved from "crisis mode" into "coping mode," I realized how fortunate I am that, at a time of trauma in my own life, I have a coping model to rely on and so much accumulated information on the various techniques and methods for coping. I hope this information will be helpful for you as well.

This book has grown out of painful life experience, my own as well as the personal experience of the people with whom I have worked as a psychologist. Most importantly, it has grown out of the experiences that all my patients, clients, and students have shared with me. As a therapist, I have been greatly privileged to be invited into the lives of people as they struggle with many of the most difficult challenges that life can send. Over many hours, we have worked together to understand what is happening in their lives and to find the ways in which they can manage most effectively. Some have had to cope with illness or the death of a loved one. Others have lived with mental illness, drug abuse, or severe conflict in the family. The crises that these people encounter often seem disastrous or nearly overwhelming. Yet there are also the more frequent challenges that we all face, at one time or another. The threats to our self-esteem are among the most common difficulties. These include the loss of a job, the anxiety associated with a difficult examination, the sorrow and questioning associated with a relationship that must end, the insecurity involved in raising a family, and the anxiety that arises when beginning anything new. In such situations, we cannot help but wonder, "Will I make it?" or "Can I cope with this one?" These are the recurring challenges that we all must be prepared to handle. Graceful mastery of these challenges of living are what this book is all about.

Second, this book has grown out of the wisdom in other books. I honor the many differing viewpoints and abundant knowledge I encountered in the formal study of psychology. These theories have been developed, on the one hand, by scientific research into human personality dynamics and, on the other hand, less formally by thoughtful reflection of experienced therapists.

I have come to realize that there has been something missing in the formal theories and research in psychology, however. We know a tremendous amount about human personality and about what makes people distressed, but there is much less written about the strengths that allow people to live gracefully. I feel it is important that we put emphasis on "what works." What I hope to offer in this volume is a synthesis of the formal psychological knowledge with the informal wisdom of people who cope. I offer a model that will help guide our choices so that we can all learn to cope more effectively.

This book comes primarily out of experience that has showed me that many people are suffering, but human beings are strong. When working in hospitals and rehabilitation centers, I have felt their sorrows and seen their courage as well. There is a saying among the staff in rehabilitation: "We are the temporarily able-bodied." That is a way to admit to ourselves that we professionals are also limited and frail. In order to get past the idea that we are separate and different from "the unfortunate ones," we often need to remind ourselves that all of us, our friends and family, everyone, will someday have major illness or other hardship to endure. None of us escapes the challenges of life.

Who I am as I write this book is the result of living through many of my own challenges and difficulties. For example, when I was sixteen, both my parents died. I had no sisters or brothers or even cousins, no family to help. That was a pretty early age to be alone in the world. I learned then about how essential it is to have supportive people around who care. Alone, without others, I found how easy it is to be caught in depression or despair. But I had memories of a loving mother who was cheerful and courageous in spite of poverty, hard work, and eventually cancer. Mom provided my first view of effective coping. When I was forty-eight, I was widowed after my husband succumbed to lung cancer. Again my life was turned upside down, and I had to draw on every strength I could find. I have faced these losses and numerous other times of trial, and I have reflected on these experiences. Somewhere in the midst of my midlife crisis, I discovered that I have become a student of coping. I wanted to know: What works? Since then I have questioned and listened and read. What I have learned about coping has enriched and deepened my understanding of life.

So this is a book about wholeness: about body, mind, and spirit. It is also about the beauty of individual people I have been privileged to know. Each of us has personal gifts, strengths, and beauty. When we learn to see these resources we possess, we can use them more effectively. We can blend more harmoniously into the whole of our environment. We can learn to cope with the challenges of life and at the same time to live more gracefully, flowing more freely with the "Tao" or stream of existence. So this book is about all of us, reflecting the lives of people who work and sometimes play, people who sorrow and people who worship. It is about the way we cope with our multitude of personal difficulties and how we transcend our individual limitations in our search for wholeness.

I want to express my gratitude to all who have shared their stories with me. From them I have learned about the uniqueness that each life represents. I have felt the subtle depths of their feelings and I have heard their dreams. I have seen the differences as each person endeavors to tell his or her own story and to find the answers to the problems that must be faced. Some of their stories appear in these pages. Some are composites where numbers of people have shared similar experiences. Others are definitely unique and, in those cases, I have received permission to write what they have told me. In all cases, I have altered identifying characteristics so that confidentiality is maintained. From all of these people I have worked with, I have gained a tremendous respect for the strength of the human spirit. Life goes on despite sometimes overwhelming difficulties. I stand in awe of the potent human will to survive.

In essence, this book is an attempt to put into words what I have learned about coping with life so that others — you who now are the readers — may broaden your perspectives and increase your options for effective coping with life. What wisdom lies in this work is a distillation of the experiences, hopes, dreams, challenges, and strengths of many people. This, in my view, is the heart of creativity. And creativity, I believe, is at the core of graceful coping.

The many facets of a comprehensive coping repertoire can be called upon to meet the various challenges we face. As we gain in understanding of the methods available, we are liberated to experiment and to discover personally what works most effectively for us in our life situations. Personal freedom is essentially linked to effective coping. Although there are moments of respite, the stresses, difficulties, and challenges arise again and again. For each of us, freedom and personal liberation are an ongoing search.

1

Six Streams: The Tao of Coping

THE HUMAN CONDITION is such that tragedy and hardship permeate life, and yet golden threads of love and hope sustain us and make us strong. When I was in Chicago, working on the head trauma unit of a rehabilitation hospital, I witnessed the tragedy of young lives broken. Day after day patients were wheeled into the ward with brain damage, usually in a comatose state as the result of sports or car accidents. I thought of my own teenage children who were healthy at home. These young patients had been normal and healthy, too, just a few days previously. I could feel the shock and grief of the parents who visited their sons and daughters. Some of these youngsters would never finish their education or never hold an ordinary job. Some would never even come out of a coma but remain in what the hospital staff called "a persistent vegetative state" for the remainder of their lives! How could these parents cope with such tragedies?

I had studied the whole range of psychological theories in graduate school — theories about personality and illness and how people cope with stress — but, as I watched and worked with these people, I began to realize that families who have major stress to deal with call upon strengths that are beyond anything we can yet measure. They call upon spirit and imagination. They learn to rely on each other, and to rely on themselves in new, deeper, more powerful ways. Every capacity that human beings have is called upon when the major crises of life hit full force.

As I thought about these families, I also began to realize there is a coherent whole about the process of coping. I began to get a sense of how the different methods of coping fit together and how they are needed for different aspects of the challenges we face. When there are big crises, we sometimes have to draw on all the strengths at once. And we cannot avoid the fact that the little problems continue even if they seem to pale in comparison to the larger life challenges. Big crises

13

bring a multitude of problems requiring a variety of approaches to deal with them. In fact, at times of economic hardship, such as we have known in the 1990s, a whole society is stressed. Problems increasingly seem to plague us, demanding the utmost in flexibility, perseverance, and stamina.

Different people take different routes in coping, but it is nevertheless useful to have an overview or a map of the terrain. I define coping very broadly. I like the metaphor of a bird's eye view, where we see that the various ways of coping are like streams flowing through a landscape. These streams come from different starting places and they may each run a different course. Some run through mountainous terrain, some through forests or perhaps flat marshy land. As I see it, there are six major streams that are all tributaries to the overall river of life that we might call "coping."

If we follow the metaphor of coping as flowing with the river of life, we can look to the Orient for understanding of how a different culture views it. In ancient China, the flow of life was called "the Tao," a sacred stream. As Jean Shinoda Bolen tells us, the Eastern mind considered the Tao the underlying connection between self and others, between self and the universe. The essential reality encompasses the power of events, dreams, and seemingly chance meetings that contain deeper meanings. The Tao can be a window on a world that is larger, more mysterious, and more whole than we imagine or can detect with our logical reasoning about concrete facts. The ancients thought that one is living right when one is in tune with the natural flow of life. For each of us the tasks of life mold and form us. We can and must adapt in some ways. At other times, we must find our own unique way through uncharted territory. Altogether, when we are in tune with the complete, ongoing flow of life, we are living harmoniously within the Tao.

In our Western way of thinking, this flow of life can be looked at in other, more scientific ways. In our society, much research has been devoted to understanding stress and ways of coping. This is our detailed, scientific way of studying the Tao or the effective ways of coping in life.

In this chapter, we will begin to look at the various methods that people use in coping. First we will think a little bit about stress and about the meaning of coping. Then I will present a model as a way to organize our thoughts. This model contains six general ways we have of coping. If you imagine the six styles of coping as six different streams, each has a different path, but they blend together in the end into an overall integrated way of effective living. To understand the art of coping we will think about some real life situations and move back and forth between the concepts and the applications of those ideas.

Coping as a Way to Master Stress

Psychologists and physicians have discovered a great deal about the effects of stress on the human organism. While we all need a certain amount of stimulation to function well, stress is cumulative and, in our fast-paced society, it is all too common that we pass the "threshold level" and find ourselves overstressed. This results in both physical and psychological distress and even dysfunction.

I often work in psychotherapy with families where there has been major stress, such as physical illness, divorce, or other traumas, and I see that there are certain patterns of behavior that help people to adjust and to minimize the negative effects of stress. These patterns are what I call "coping styles." *Coping refers to all the healthy ways, both conscious and unconscious, that a person uses in adjusting to environmental demands, whether great or small.* Coping styles are related to our personality types and consequently they vary from one person to the next. It is beneficial to understand your own coping style; and it is important to know that other people (specifically, other family members) may benefit from using coping methods entirely different from the ones that you use yourself.

Some coping styles are internal, that is, these methods of coping are based on what occurs within our psyches. These internal methods are the ways in which we use our thinking abilities (planning, analyzing, synthesizing information), regulate our emotions (especially anxiety, anger, and depression), or call upon spiritual resources to strengthen us for the challenges we face. Other methods are external. These external methods include those in which we gather information, act in the environment, and draw on the social support of others who are available to offer help. Keeping physically fit is also vital, especially for maintaining the stamina we need for crisis situations or long-term challenges. See Table 1 on the following page to help you get that bird's eye view of the varieties of coping options. This model is key to understanding your own coping styles so that you can choose more wisely which methods to draw upon when stress occurs in your life. I will describe and develop the six coping styles more fully as we go along.

TABLE 1. A MODEL OF COPING STYLES

Internal Coping Styles   *External Coping Styles*

COPING STYLES FOCUSED ON HARMONIZING EMOTIONS

1. Internal regulation of emotion (especially using imagery and participation
in creative expression to control
and relieve anxiety, anger, and
depression)

2. Seeking social support (developing
good nourishing relationships with
others)

COPING STYLES ORIENTED TOWARD HEALTHY LIVING

3. Spiritual practices (prayer,
meditation, contemplation)

4. Maintaining physical fitness
(strengths, flexibility, relaxation,
and harmony in the body)

COPING STYLES FOCUSED ON SOLVING PROBLEMS

5. Thinking (planning, analyzing,
synthesizing information)

6. Gathering information and acting in
the environment

Not everyone uses all six styles, certainly not all the time. But having a broad array of methods allows for flexibility and choice. In order
to see how some of these different aspects of coping may fit together,
here is an example of a life situation that requires the utmost flexibility
in stress management and coping: I first met the man I'll call "Henry"
when he came for a therapy group in the neurology department of a
large metropolitan hospital. At that time, he was sixty years old, a
heavy-set man, slightly balding, with a big smile and a big heart. People
felt good when Henry was wheeled into the room in his wheelchair. We
all felt inspired whenever he shared his ideas. He was willing to talk
about his own life story because he had discovered a lot about coping
and what he said seemed to be helpful to others.

Henry has had multiple sclerosis (MS) for over forty years. MS is a
chronic disease in which the insulation around some of the neurons of
the nervous system is mysteriously eaten away by an autoimmune process. This means that what should be a solid protective sheath for the
nerve cells may end up looking like Swiss cheese. The holes in the protective sheath result in poor conduction of the electrical currents. This
causes a wide variety of symptoms that range from mild sensory abnormalities to severe disabilities. Some patients have only mild symptoms
throughout their lives. Others have progressive deterioration of many

important physical functions. In terms of physical degeneration, Henry was one of the unlucky ones.

In young adulthood, while Henry was studying for his doctorate in engineering, he began to develop multiple sclerosis in his spinal chord. Fortunately, the neurons in his brain were unaffected, but he had increasing physical disablement that prevented him from completing the fieldwork and data collection for his doctoral dissertation. His disappointment was acute, but Henry was a man who was not easily daunted. He was able to secure a faculty position at a small university where he taught engineering and computer courses. He has retained that position throughout his adult life.

Over the years, Henry developed many of the most severe symptoms of MS. When he lost the use of his lower limbs, he was confined to a wheelchair. Bladder and bowel problems plagued him periodically, requiring repeated hospitalizations. Henry also recounts the sorrow of the time in his life when he lost capacity for sexual functioning. He could no longer feel those tantalizing sensations. His marriage suffered; when sexual love-making could no longer be part of their married life, a time of grief prevailed. With the stress in the family, his two grown children suffered as well. Another major loss occurred when he had to give up swimming. Henry loved to swim. For a long time, that had been such a pleasurable form of exercise. No longer could he relish the moments when he was let down into the pool to paddle around, letting the cool water float him.

With this progressive disease, Henry gradually lost the use of his arms as well as legs. By age sixty, he was quadriplegic. The tragedy of a major progressive illness has been his fate throughout most of his adult years. Nonetheless, Henry has lived a rich, full life. He continues to cope with his disability by using an array of intellectual, social, and spiritual resources.

Henry recounts memories of his father, a rabbi who came to this country after suffering many hardships in Europe. Henry's father was a courageous role model who taught him about strength, perseverance, and undaunted trust in God. Spiritual strengths are passed on both by words and deeds. From his dad, Henry gained a sense of life's core meaning and value.

Henry also was gifted with a fine brain. He continues to teach and has received numerous awards including "Teacher of the Year." He uses all his intellectual capacities to the fullest. As his disabilities increased, he was able to design special equipment to allow him as much independent functioning as possible. When he could no longer write on the blackboard, he used overhead projectors to teach. When he could no longer use his hands, he designed "sip-and-puff" mechanisms to control his wheelchair and worked with rehabilitation specialists to obtain instruments that would allow him maximum self-control. Now, in the later stages of his illness, he uses a specially designed van and employs a home health aide to transport him to work.

In addition to his own intellectual and spiritual resources, Henry has a capacity to relate to others, in a mutually supportive way. He cares for others and he has learned to express his feelings. In a multiple sclerosis support group, he shares his strengths, fears, and sorrows with others who have similar problems. Because of his courage and determination, he is an inspiration for other MS patients. He is also a role model for his students and even for the MS medical staff. He elicits respect because of the very problems that he has overcome. He inspires by example.

Henry also gives much of himself. He is psychologically a strong and powerful man. Part of his strength is his ability to acknowledge those situations in which he is powerless; in those conditions he is able to seek and to receive the help he needs. He is able to use assertiveness to the full extent, when the situation requires it, yet he is also able to acknowledge and to accept his dependence on others. In spite of his disabilities, he is aware and in control of many aspects of his life. He lives life to the fullest. Despite quadriplegia, he has continued to work at a full-time faculty position and plans to do so until the normal retirement age. For Henry a sense of mastery comes from knowing that he is coping well with the challenges he faces.

Although fate has not been easy on him, Henry is a remarkable person who copes with severe disability by consciously using a wide range of coping styles. He is a man of intelligence, cultivation, and sophistication. In order for us to begin to catalog, to understand, and to organize the specific methods he uses, we can see that his major strength is intellectual and he relies most readily on coping methods aimed at solving realistic problems. Analyzing his other coping methods, we see that although he gets depressed from time to time, he has been able to pull himself out of the doldrums with the help of emotional support that he receives in his group, from his wife, and in other relationships. While he sought to maintain his health as long as possible through regular exercise such as swimming, he eventually had to forego that form of coping. His regular visits to physicians have been aimed at aborting and minimizing the negative effects of MS flare-ups. As his physical limitations inevitably progressed, it has become increasingly clear that his spiritual strength, philosophy, and healthy attitudes have been the major sustaining factors undergirding his life. Like a well-engineered building, Henry is a man built with a solid substructure. The variety of coping strengths on which he draws is what allows him to live as fully as possible. It is this very capacity to cope gracefully in the face of major disablement that makes this man the extraordinary person that he is. His strength of character is justifiably admired by people who know him.

Coping Theory

Many of us who work in the helping professions find that the idea of coping is a useful way of organizing our thoughts about what it means to be psychologically healthy. What works well tends to keep us happy and makes for harmonious relationships with others. There are many approaches that psychologists take, but most would agree that coping is best when we behave in realistic and flexible ways. We can all recognize that coping is effective when it solves problems and reduces stress. One major criterion professionals use to define effective coping has to do with how accurate a person is in judging reality. A person needs to address real problems in a realistic way in order to find good solutions.

Psychologist Norma Haan has written extensively about the differences between good coping and the more defensive attitudes that distort reality. We human beings all have attitudes and patterns of behavior that create difficulties for ourselves and others. We seem to need to learn what doesn't work before we are willing to make the effort to change to more effective ways of living. For this reason, in psychotherapy we often need to devote a great deal of effort to exploring the negative or ineffective ways of thinking, feeling, and behaving. These ways are counterproductive and defensive.

When we distort reality, we have lost the power it takes to change ourselves and to find ways to adapt to life as it is. We are no longer in tune with the Tao. We distort reality also when we project our feelings onto others and believe that "all the negative stuff is out there," or when we deny that there really are any problems at all. We also distort reality when we think, feel, and behave the way we did in childhood. If we are caught in the "inner child of the past," we are usually not behaving appropriately for the realities of today.

On the other hand, when we are coping well we have assessed reality accurately and we are flexible in our choice of actions. Our ways of thinking, feeling, and behaving are productive and mature. Leading psychologists at the Menninger Foundation studied coping styles and came to the conclusion that mature coping includes the following patterns of behavior:

- *Humor.* Being able to lighten up and laugh at yourself or at the situation.

- *Weeping.* Being able to cry about the realistic difficulties and losses you are facing.

- *Talking emotions out.* Being able to put words to your feelings and sharing them with people who understand your situation and accept you as you are.

- *Working off energy.* Finding physical activity and tasks that require effort in order to use up the excess energy that you have developed in your stressful situation.

- *Thinking problems through.* Being able to organize your thoughts clearly and make rational decisions about how to improve the situation you face.

- *Self-control.* Being able to know your feelings but to control any behavior (such as aggression) that would only make matters worse.

Harvard psychiatrist George Valliant would add to the list of mature coping strategies:

- *Altruism.* Being able and willing to do for others.

- *Sublimation.* Being able to transform inappropriate impulses into energy that you can use in socially acceptable ways (for example, using the energy generated by anger to work on a project such as an ecological clean-up).

- *Suppression of unwanted emotions.* Being able to calm your feelings and deintensify them. (Suppression differs from repression, in which feelings are pushed into the unconscious. Repression is not a mature coping strategy and generally results in a multitude of negative consequences.)

- *Anticipation of events.* Being able to predict what is likely to happen so that you have time to preplan and decide on your strategies for coping.

Another way of looking at coping behaviors has developed recently in response to the public interest in stress and its effects on health. Richard Lazarus and Susan Folkman are researchers who led the Berkeley Stress and Coping Project. These psychologists think of coping as an antidote to stress. They have expressed their view that the most important component of coping is the thought process by which a person describes the situation to himself or herself. In their research, Lazarus and Folkman found that people who describe their situation as a "challenge" are inclined to have better morale, to function more effectively, and consequently to have better overall health than those people who view their life difficulties more negatively in terms of a "threat." So the way we label our stresses has significant impact on how well we cope with them. If we see them as "challenges," we have a far better chance of overcoming the difficulties and coping well. This subtle difference in labeling allows us opportunity to gain a sense of mastery. I will say more about mastery later on.

Lazarus and Folkman are current leaders in the field of coping research, and they deserve credit for recognizing that coping methods various people choose may be either "problem-focused" or "emotion-focused." They realized that people differ in their style of coping, with some aiming primarily toward solution of an external problem and others more oriented toward regulation of the internal emotions that result from a problem being present. I agree with these researchers that the problem-focused and emotion-focused styles of coping are important distinctions to make. I feel that they have not gone far enough, however, and so in this book you will find additional coping styles and a model that is more extensive in its overview of the coping options that we can and do use when we have major stresses in our lives.

Stress and Stressors

Belinda works an average of sixty hours per week at her job as systems analyst. Her brother, who is equally bright, is unemployed. Their parents are worried about both of them. The stress of overwork or of underemployment affects everyone in a family system. Stress has become a very popular topic these days. We see it all around us: incredibly long work weeks, threatened layoffs at many places of employment, and fear of economic instability or unemployment. We have all come to recognize that stress is an aspect of living, and we know that it can affect our health. Many of us have had opportunities to read about or to attend workshops on stress management. I find it is helpful when we clarify the meaning of stress in terms of some of the original physiological research and recent discoveries. (You will find more about stress and its effects on the body in chapter 5.)

The early researchers were William Cannon, who in 1929 described some of the key emotional mechanisms in the mind-body connection, and Hans Selye, who defined "stress" in 1956 and identified its physiological components. The findings of these physiologists led to an enormous amount of scientific interest and many clinical discoveries about the effect of stress on the body.

According to Selye, there is a specific sequence that occurs in your body. First, there is a stressful event. He calls this event a "stressor" and describes it as any event that impinges itself on the human organism. Stressors make demands on your body, causing it to readjust. Second, as a result of this demand for adjustment, "stress" occurs. Selye describes stress as "the nonspecific response of the body to any demand." That is, stress is the biochemical and physiological change that occurs in your body as a result of the stressor. Third, when there are too many stressors, the level of stress in your body may exceed your ability to adapt, and the result is vulnerability to physical illness. You are then likely to suffer the pathological consequences of too much stress, that is, you may contract any one of a variety of diseases. Or, if you already have an organic weakness such as chronic pain or illness, this condition may worsen.

Today most people use the general term "stress" to refer both to the "stressors" that Selye described and to the actual physical effects on the body. I will follow that informal convention from here on, but it is useful for us to realize that the body's response is to specific agents from the external world or to emotions that also can serve as stressors. The key point is: *stress is quantitative, and too much leads to body breakdown!*

Physicians and psychologists have been actively involved in trying to understand how the body responds to stress in order to find ways to help people to buffer themselves from the effects of too much stress. Recent research discoveries have helped us to understand the importance of psychological responses. We now know that pathological changes occurring in the body are not directly caused by an aversive stressor but, more generally, by the inability of the body to deal with the stressor. What one needs to address, then, is the problem that causes the stress. So we know that the effect of stress is mediated by the coping ability of the person. This means that the situation is not totally hopeless. You can combat unavoidable stress in your life by increasing your ability to cope!

Your body is most likely to become dysfunctional if either of two conditions occur. First, you can expect physical damage to occur if your coping efforts are entirely unsuccessful. Or, second, even if you are somewhat successful in coping with some aspect of your problem, you may suffer some physical breakdown if you have created a real *imbalance* in your life. When a lack of balance is created, one system within the body overfunctions in order to compensate for another disabled system. The good news is that coping can be effective as a buffer against stress and can save us from a great deal of unnecessary physical pain and illness. If you can maintain a balance in your life, and if you can cope successfully with your environmental challenges, you will experience little or no stress in your body. When you are coping successfully, you will tend to view your challenges as only minimally stressful. Then you will have less likelihood of negative effects on your health. You are likely to feel more in tune with the Tao.

On the other hand, we must not punish ourselves or others for being sick! It is important to remember that every disease in itself causes stress. As Selye pointed out, any disease imposes demands for adaptation. And, in turn, stress plays some role in the development of every disease. We must be careful not to add to the burdens of physical illness by labeling the patient psychologically inadequate. At some time or another, we all get sick. Illness and eventual death are inevitable. We can use the stress concept and the coping ideas to help reduce the ill effects, but none of us is ever able totally to remove all stress and imbalance from our lives.

If we could do the impossible, remove all stress, we would not be happy with the result! That would mean there would be no change and no variety in our lives. Under such stagnant circumstances, life would hardly be worth living; we would be psychologically dead. So we must admit that in order to provide change, variety, and vibrancy in our lives, we must accept some stress as a result. The aim is to keep a sense of balance and harmony and an optimum, rather than an excessive, level of stress. This will allow our bodies to adapt most easily.

Coping with Change

Change in the world around often means that we must adapt to dramatically new circumstances. Even economic or political changes that occur on the other side of the world may ultimately impact each of us and require lifestyle changes. Unemployment, for example, may be one of those changes that comes along unexpectedly. Any such change puts many challenges before us. Whenever we encounter a major change in life, a multitude of new events place demands on our own mind-body systems. So change is, almost by definition, stressful. Even when we welcome it, change disrupts stability. Coping with change requires us to understand and manage the inevitable stress that occurs. Frequently we can modulate the amount of stress by managing the amount of change we are ready to undertake.

Sigmund Freud frequently referred to what he called "the vicissitudes of life." By this he meant the unexpectedly changing circumstances of life that require us to make constant adaptations. Yet change is an integral part of human dynamics. That is, who we are depends on how we adapt to the changing external and internal circumstances of our lives. Especially in our fast-paced society, how we adapt to change is a central challenge of adult life.

Change may sometimes feel like loss, or even failure. Often we have to let go of past accomplishments and times of comfortable living. Do you remember those changes that have felt like wrenching loss? Those times you had to let go of a mutually supportive relationship? Or the loss of a group in which you felt accepted? At times in life, you may have to let go of a favorite role you have had — a role that makes you feel respected and good about yourself. Letting go of a respected work role may also leave you feeling threatened about loss of financial security. When these losses mount up, your sense of dignity may be weakened. You may need to renegotiate the meanings and values that you use to set your goals in life. You will undoubtedly even need to reestablish your sense of self-identity from time to time. Each of us initially consolidates a sense of identity in late adolescence, but we must reestablish a sense of who we are in adulthood whenever life changes spark major upheaval that affects all aspects of our personalities.

On the other hand, change may feel like improvement. The idea of growth and development implies that throughout adulthood we are aiming at a process of fulfillment or completion. In some sense, we expect later stages to be better than the earlier, less mature times in our lives. It is important to realize that any given change may be for better or for worse. Professionals who work with people who are undergoing traumatic events, such as a fire or other natural disaster, have learned that crises may lead to either negative or positive consequences. When we undergo crises, it may lead to a deterioration and worsening of our abilities to function effectively. Or the crisis may lead to improved functioning, growth, and enhanced realization of our potentials. The crisis is a disequilibrium, or turning point. It all depends on how well we cope. We all know people, such as Henry, who are able to rise to whatever challenge presents itself in life.

Sometimes a crisis even feels like an attack on the very core of your psychological being. What fate requires of you then is a redefinition of yourself, a rediscovery of meaning, and a renewal of your commitment to what you choose as most important in your life. After getting over such a rocky transition place, you may have changed course a bit, but you are likely to feel more in tune with the Tao, the flow of life, once again.

Inner or Outer?

As we saw, Selye described stress as the result of assault on the human organism from either internal or external sources. You could probably list dozens of *external* sources of stress that affect you everyday. For example, there are physical stressors such as excess heat or cold that require your body to adjust. If you have allergies, you are well aware of the troublesome effect of pollen that reaches your respiratory system. If someone assaults you with a weapon or any kind of a pain-producing instrument, the effect is considerable stress on your body. A large number of medical procedures are physically invasive and therefore create stress at the very same time they are attempting to diagnose or heal some other condition.

On the home front, you may be stressed by an argument with your spouse or with your teenage son. At work you may have too many tasks to accomplish in the time available, or you may have a disagreeable and irate boss. These are all well-known external sources of stress, but their effect can also be heightened by internal processes as well.

Internal sources of stress result from psychological attempts to deal with life. Great inner turmoil can be created when we get caught into conflictual thinking. For example, consider Hamlet's conflict: "To be or not to be?" That question was a profound source of anguish, which Shakespeare so eloquently narrated. Every day we all have lesser conflicts that take up a great deal of our psychic energy and strength. Simple goal conflicts, such as whether to go to the grocery store or stay home and do the laundry, are among the low-level stressors that can sometimes nag at us from within.

Any important decisions create internal conflict until they are resolved. We also have ongoing inner conflicts such as how to be a good parent. How strict or permissive to be? How to communicate caring? How to respond when another disagrees or has differing needs from our own? Many of these various conflicts come about in the warfare between the part of ourselves that wants to be upright, honest, respected, and diligent (those aspects that Freud called "the superego") and the other parts of us that want to play, to relax, to have comfort, and to have it now (Freud's "id").

In addition to internal conflicts, another internal source of stress comes about as a result of unwanted emotions. Many times we get angry or anxious because of something happening in the external environment, but sometimes we don't let those feelings go and they continue to plague us from within, creating our own internal source of stress. When we are unable to relax our minds or unable to rid ourselves of emotions, we are caught in a pattern of internal stress.

A young man came to me recently with a problem that involved both internal and external sources of stress. He was a sensitive, artistic type of person but had been working for several years as a teacher in a tough inner-city high school. He hated the discipline problems he encountered and wanted to change his career. He clearly saw the external stressors in the school system: rebellious kids, disgruntled faculty, a harsh and punitive administration. He began to search for a different job. So far he had not been successful in finding one, and the new school year was fast approaching. While he continued the job hunt, he began to work also on the internal sphere of his own psyche. He began to ask: If he had to return to his old teaching position, how could he cope? What could he do to change himself so that the coming year would be different and better than the last? What attitudes could he change? How could he reduce his anger? His anxiety? His tendency to feel inadequate? How could he plan his behaviors so that he would be more likely to be successful in the external world of the inner-city school? Both inner and outer sources of stress were present. Until he could obtain another job, this young man needed to adjust his coping style so that he could call on both inner and outer resources.

Now we've seen that stress can originate in the environment or it can be perpetuated by conflicts or residual emotions that hang on within our psyches. The source of stress, in part, guides our choice of coping style. When we clearly identify the source of our stress, we can have much freer choice about how to combat it. Self-awareness helps us choose. We can aim our coping efforts primarily toward the external world or we can work on the internal world of the psyche. Inner and outer aspects of coping efforts are both important. When you recognize your stress and its sources you are better able to choose your way of coping.

If you are an extrovert or a managerial type of person, you may be more inclined to attempt first to solve problems in the environment. If you are an introvert or contemplative by nature, you are more apt to look inwardly first, working your way through the problem in the intrapsychic world of thought, imagination, and spirit before attempting to act in the environment. It is important to realize, however, that each of us has the capacity to use both internal and external coping mechanisms. In fact, we will need both.

Where to Focus?

In addition to inner and outer aspects of coping, there are three general ways we can aim or focus our attempts at coping. First, we can use our intellectual capacities to identify and solve problems. This is what psychologists call "problem-focused coping." Second, we can approach the challenges that face us by exploring and altering the emotions that are generated in us or in others. We call this approach "emotion-focused coping." Third, we can approach life from the positive perspective of holistic health. This third approach is oriented toward both physical and spiritual well-being. Its aim is to prevent dysfunction. This "health-oriented coping" is appropriate at any time, whether stress levels are high or low. When our aim is health-oriented, we are more directly following the purpose of attuning ourselves with the Tao. As one cancer patient said, "That's where we want to get: beyond merely coping!"

I think often of Henry, the quadriplegic patient I described earlier. He has managed to master his extremely limited physical condition by using his intellect for problem-solving (problem-focused coping). He enriches his life and manages his emotions by relating personably with all the people he encounters — his caregivers, fellow patients, students, colleagues, and friends (emotion-focused coping). But his greatest gift is his ability to go beyond "merely coping" to a level of effective living that inspires respect from all who know of him. This transcendence of problems and emotional difficulties and emergence into graceful living is what makes Henry so unique. His extraordinary capacity to cope is a result of his utmost striving with his physical world, and his sense of meaning and purpose, all of which reveal his deep spiritual roots and essential courage (health-oriented coping). Henry is doing a lot more than just hanging in there. He is beyond merely coping and is living each day creatively.

For any of us, the way we focus our coping efforts depends on the particular difficulties that we face. When we look at the whole range of coping strategies we will, of course, need to consider the specific nature of the stress before we choose. Even so, we each tend to have our favorite coping methods. Some methods we may overuse, while others we may neglect. By and large, most people have a limited repertoire of coping methods, and we tend automatically to choose those methods that have worked well for us in similar circumstances in the past. Personality is a major factor in determining choice of coping methods. As a child grows she experiences life's stresses and begins to develop ways of coping that fit both with her personality and with the challenges she must master. In later life, when her responsibilities and stresses may be great, the adult draws on what she already knows about "what works." People who cope most effectively with the greatest demands that life sends are those who have a broad array of skills and a keen perception of themselves, of others, and of the nature of the challenges at hand.

Coping styles begin to develop early in life. As parents, we have much to teach our children when we model effective coping behavior. Our coping styles are related both to our genetic make-up and, more importantly, to the experiences we have encountered during life. It is also good to remember that we can all continue to grow in our capacity to meet the challenges of life more gracefully. It seems to me that at the heart of wisdom lies the sense of the growing ability to master life's ongoing difficulties.

As another example of the varying ways people in the same family may approach their common problems, let's look at Sarah and her family: Sarah's handsome, professional parents were both very concerned about her when they decided that divorce was the only alternative for them to change their troubled family. They wondered how Sarah would cope with the distress that they all were feeling. Sarah was now in her senior year of high school. She was the youngest of three children, and she would soon be the last to leave the family nest. Sarah pretended that nothing was bothering her. Since she was quite athletic, she increased the time she went to the skating rink. She even thought wistfully about competitive skating and wondered if she would have had a chance for the Olympics if she had started earlier.

Sarah's mother was finishing up a master's degree, planning soon to begin a career as a counselor. She urged Sarah to talk about her feelings, but mother-daughter communications always seemed to get bogged down whenever the subject of the divorce or Sarah's father came up. Sarah just couldn't seem to talk to her mother about her deepest feelings of hurt and fear. Sarah would soon be going off to college. She would then be on her own, and it was terrifying for her to realize that her family would not be there to return to. Certainly she knew it would never be the same again.

Sarah's Dad loved her very much. He remembered the days when he used to go out and throw around footballs with Sarah and her two brothers. It seemed to him that the last ten years had gone by so quickly and he had let pass so many opportunities to be with his daughter. Sometimes he felt he hardly knew her anymore. He was a practical man. Recently, it seemed that dealing with the demands of making a living had taken up so much of his energy. He had been too distressed to recognize that the family break-up was inevitable. The anger between his wife and himself was unreconcilable. They had tried a few sessions of marital counseling and it all seemed futile to him. The anger was too deep, too intense. But with the anger, there was sadness, too.

He didn't let himself feel too much of that. He turned instead to thinking about the practical problems they would have to work through. But the sorrow remained. The worst of it was the feeling that he was losing his daughter. He worried about her and how she would be affected. Would she be able to cope?

This situation is not unusual with a divorce during the children's high school or college years. As it turned out, Sarah maintained her "stiff upper lip" until she got off to college. She relied a lot on her friends but seldom told them how troubled she really felt. She dated and broke up with several boyfriends, always fearing that if she got "too serious," she might end up in a marriage having as much pain as she saw in her parents'.

Finally, after a friend had died in a freak swimming accident during sophomore year of college, Sarah started psychotherapy. At first, she did not tell either of her parents that she was getting help. They had been prodding her, but she needed this to be *her* therapy. Eventually, she was able to resolve many of her feelings of loss and anger associated with the divorce. She had to separate from her parents (as do all older adolescents) and still retain her contacts and sense of connection with each of them.

The coping styles used most frequently in Sarah's family differed for each of the family members. Sarah's mother used "emotion-focused coping" and found that, for her, talking things out with supportive friends was the best way to deal with her troubled feelings. Sarah's father, on the other hand, was far more inclined to use "problem-focused coping." He was an intelligent, thoughtful man who could handle practical matters well, but he often had difficulties with emotions. Sarah herself was reluctant to express her feelings in the family. She turned instead to sports and to her peer group. She did finally benefit tremendously from the opportunity to express her feelings to a therapist, but she had to be ready. It had to be her own decision and her commitment to finding a way to a fuller life.

In most families, the coping styles vary considerably. Each person needs to have a variety of coping techniques available to call upon when needed. It is vital to remember that we can all grow in our abilities to cope effectively! Equally important, we must recognize that another person's coping methods may be very effective for *that person*, even if they are not the methods we would use.

Learning to cope is a broadening, growthful process whereby each

TABLE 2. SIX STREAMS OF COPING

	Internal	*External*
Emotion-focused Coping:	1. The Underground River	2. Social Support (Smoothing the Way)
Health-oriented Coping:	3. The Way of the Spirit	4. The Body's Ways
Problem-focused Coping:	5. The Inner Computer and Its Ways	6. Action Research (The Warrior's Way)

person matures, throughout life, into more effective living. Our essential aim is to deepen our understanding and broaden the scope of the coping strategies that we have available. At this point, I want to put together these various perspectives on coping in order to give you a unified, comprehensive picture.

The Bird's Eye View

A wide variety of coping methods exist, each of which is useful. Like streams flowing toward the river, each may take a different route but still end as tributary to the same river. If we imagine ourselves flying over the landscape, we see that some streams flow over similar terrain. Some streams have adapted well to flat marshy land. Others are rushing over rocky places between high cliffs. Some of the tributaries may join one another. Each adapts to its surroundings. Each flows naturally with its own inner force.

Let's look now, through our Western psychological perspective, at how these streams relate to one another. One way of organizing the vast array of information about various coping methods is to put the categories together. So far, I have outlined two different dimensions. First we looked at the inner versus the outer dimension. The second dimension includes three aspects: problem-focused, emotion-focused, and health-oriented coping. Now if we put these two dimensions together to form what scientists would describe as a two-dimensional model, the 2 x 3 cells of the model correspond to the six streams that I have been referring to as metaphor. When we look at each of the six streams, we can think about coping styles in terms of the focus or aim, and the internal versus external location of coping efforts. See Table 2 above to help you keep the overview in mind. The chapters that follow will explain the six streams or coping styles more completely.

2

The Way
of the Underground River

AS WE BEGIN TO EXAMINE more closely the methods that are available to help with emotion-focused coping, we look first to the fertile, unconscious resources of the inner world. Here lies the secret source of creativity that enables us to cope with our sometimes troublesome emotions. In this chapter we will look to processes governed by the right hemisphere of the brain, to music and the arts, and primarily to the manifestations of the deep unconscious as they arise in imagery, dreams, and self-hypnosis.

There are many layers of the psyche, and the terrain has only partially been mapped. Images are the usual language of the unconscious world, so as we learn to read their language, images guide, educate, and comfort us. Ordinary images or fantasies may help us cope, or they may be detrimental. For example, when we imagine the worst, our fantasies may take us into emotional turmoil; or fantasies may take us off into escapes from that everyday world. But self-affirmative images, and imagining positive outcomes, will prepare us for success and effective coping. There is also a deeper level to the imaginal world. Below the level of ordinary fantasy, images can be very influential on how we feel and behave. We can use images at this deeper level to create or to contact the imaginal space in which we have greater freedom. Deeper yet we find the dreamworld. The underground river nourishes us every night. We will begin this inward journey by getting a feel for uses of daytime imagery.

Imagery in Daily Life

At the dinner table I sat talking with two salesmen. Brad was Irish, middle-aged, medium build, very fit and hardy. His son-in-law, Chris, was a huge mountain of a man, of Swiss descent, dark and handsome in a rugged kind of way. We talked of many things, but eventually the topic that drew us together was the fascinating question of visual imagery. We began to discuss how people consciously use imagery to cope with various challenges of life. Brad was a highly successful entrepreneur and national sales manager for a major company. Chris sold sporting goods and had just returned home following a near-fatal attack of a rare blood disease. As we talked I sensed how we were all energized when we began to realize the impact of the imaginal world in helping these two men deal with the challenges they have faced. Each of us had spontaneously encountered and used visual imagery very differently. That night I came to realize that both internal and external events could be managed more effectively through the use of visual imagery.

Brad told us that he had been practicing visual imagery for years, as preparation for what might be difficult events. For example, in his high school days he had spent Friday nights preparing for the upcoming football games. He would visualize the whole game: his part in it, the way each of the plays would go. When the real game occurred the next day, of course it was not exactly the same as his imagining, but he felt prepared, "up" and ready to fight the battle for all it was worth. Imagining victory and all the steps that would be required to achieve it helped him to be the best possible team player. Although he was only a medium-sized man, he was a valued player and captain of both high school and college football teams.

Public speaking is another arena in which visual imagery can provide useful preparation. Brad told us that he runs through any speech fully in his mind before ever speaking it aloud. He also uses the power of his imagination to prepare for workshop presentations. He prepares by imagining the scene, complete with questions from the audience and the "feel" of the room (as he visualizes it). He imagines where he will stand, how he will use the visual aids, and how the day will flow. He is never nervous to get up before an audience as long as he has had adequate preparation time to run through the event in his mind thoroughly. This is Brad's conscious choice. Using visualization to imagine a successful presentation is the most important stress-reducing aspect of his preparation.

Chris, the younger salesman, added to our dinner conversation by telling his own experiences with visual imagery. When he was a teenager, he had learned meditation from a girlfriend. He experimented and found the "special place" that he most enjoyed visualizing was that totally attuned moment in riding the surf, that eternal moment when the huge blue-green wave curls overhead and one soars forward in complete peace and harmony with nature and with oneself. This imagery was immensely helpful for him under stressful circumstances. When he was drafted and had to deal with the harsh realities of the Vietnam war, he used the image of the wave to cope with pain and fear. Twice he was shot and wounded. Each time he used the peaceful imagery of the inner wave to help him come through and remain psychologically sound.

Experience with meditation and the use of visual imagery can provide good background for the times of peak stress, such as those times in life when we must cope with serious injury or illness. Chris next spoke poignantly of his recent illness, a serious blood-thinning disease called ITP (idiopathic thrombocytopenic purpura). His blood platelets were continually attacked by a mysterious autoimmune process that physicians at the veterans' hospital attributed to his prolonged exposure to Agent Orange, the chemical defoliant used in Vietnam. They gave him steroids, but his cardiovascular and immune systems were badly out of balance, and for months he hovered on the brink of death.

A family member sent a copy of Bernie Siegel's book *Love, Medicine and Miracles* and a tape on the use of imagery for cancer patients. From his hospital room, Chris began a renewed fight for life. He first went through relaxation procedures. Then he started visualizing, beginning at his toes and working upward. He imagined pulling all the "sludge" up and out from his bloodstream. He said, "Since there was no one place to focus the healing energies, all I could do was imagine cleansing out the whole bloodstream. I'd just visualize pulling up the sludge, bit by bit, until I could expel it from the top of my head." (Other patients have been equally successful in imagining a healing golden flow starting at the top of the head and working downward to the toes.) Month by month, this young man imagined cleansing his body of the toxic foreign elements that endangered his life. Like cancer patients, he viewed what was attacking him as an enemy from inside. His persistent efforts at visualization, along with the love and support he received from family and friends, helped to unlock the door to healing. Visualization was a key technique. He began to get better. The doctors were puzzled by his recovery, as puzzled as they had been by the mysterious onset and intractable characteristics of his disease.

Conscious visualization can be effective, whether the field of endeavor is health, education, business, athletics, or the creative arts. When we visualize, we communicate from our mind to our body. In the process of forming images and thoughts in our mind, whether consciously or unconsciously, we transmit them to the body as signals or commands. Researchers have not yet identified exactly *how* this process of mind-body communication occurs, but we have ample convincing evidence that powerful channels of energy and control do exist. We do know that the right hemisphere of the brain, with its image-based functioning, exerts a powerful influence on all our behavior. And we are now learning that we can consciously evoke the images that will help us to cope.

As I reflected at the dinner conversation with these two salesmen, I became aware that use of visual imagery may be a lot more common as a coping mechanism than most of us realize. We know that it can operate on an unconscious level, as well as sometimes being conscious. I shared my own experience in research into visual imagery, which provides one example of the mechanism by which imagery can help us to cope.

Research with the Unconscious

When gathering resources for my doctoral dissertation. I came across a book in which psychologists Seymour Fisher and Sidney Cleveland summarized their discoveries about some remarkable differences in body-image symbolism. For their research, they had used the Rorschach inkblots and several other projective tests. We know that when people view an ambiguous inkblot, they tend to project onto that vague stimulus an image that is coming from their own life experience and from their unconscious. Fisher and Cleveland found that there are significant relationships between people's perceptions of the inkblots and real or imagined events that occur in their physical bodies.

Now *body image* is both a visual and a kinesthetic experience of oneself. It has both conscious and unconscious aspects. Body image is related to the way you perceive yourself in the world: how you look, how you feel, the sensations you experience when you move. Body image is a lifelong, cumulative experience, including memories of you, for example, as the "little girl with freckles and braids," the "slim college student," the "pregnant mother." All these memories of who you were and how you looked are incorporated into your present perceptions as you look in the mirror. Body image represents your sense of self and how you are differentiated from others. It is determined by your experience of your boundaries in relation to others. Body image is how you own your unique self in the world. There is a sense of "this is who I am; this is where I begin and end." Along with body image as being "distinctly you," you have an expectation of being a consistent self in different situations.

One of the most universal aspects of body image is the boundary between the way you experience your body — with all its sensations, thoughts, and emotions — and what is external to it. Your psychological boundary defines who you are, as you respond to the environment. The boundary of your body image is also concerned with your assessments of your vulnerability to outside forces and your resiliency in protecting yourself. A significant aspect of how well you can cope is related to how vulnerable, how defended, and how resilient you feel yourself to be.

Fisher and Cleveland found that certain medical patients, because they feel particularly vulnerable, tend to respond to the Rorschach inkblots with defended, armor-like perceptions. That is, when they view the Rorschach, the patients tend to give unique responses that involved special emphasis on the boundary-defining qualities of objects. When shown the ambiguous inkblots, they would tend to "see" protective, containing, covering, or decorative surface images, such as a helmet, a cave, a cape, or a finely decorated vase. Fisher and Cleveland called these "body-image barrier" perceptions. These barrier perceptions are symbolic of protection, defense, and coping. In the inkblot tests, barrier responses contrast to "penetration" perceptions, which emphasize the open aspects of body-image symbols, including the wounded, vulnerable ways we sometimes feel.

In the body-image research that I then conducted, we studied multiple sclerosis patients at early, middle, and late stages of their illness. MS is usually a slow, degenerative, sometimes crippling disease, and I wanted to learn how patients defend themselves psychologically and how they cope over the long term. We found that patients in the initial stages of the disease showed projective responses with high "penetration" perceptions, that is, patients' sense of vulnerability and anxieties about their bodies were highest in the first few years after diagnosis.

Over time, as patients began to age and to become experienced in coping with this degenerative disease, their "barrier" responses increased. At an unconscious level, this meant that the body-image barrier seems to form as a defense against the woundedness a patient feels when a disease such as MS is active in the body.

There are two implications that result from this psychological study. First, we can now realize that unconscious imagery goes on naturally within patients to help them in coping with serious disease of long duration. It appears that the unconscious body image is altered in such a way that a certain protective shield is formed. It is as though the unconscious subtle body automatically wraps itself up in bandages to protect its wounded parts, to allow them to rest in maximum comfort, and to allow healing to occur.

The second implication is that what occurs unconsciously can also be made conscious. You can call upon any of your imaginal resources; that is, you have the power to evoke the image. You can consciously use such body-image protectiveness to help you cope with accident, illness, or even other kinds of threats. This is a very practical matter. Imagine, for example, a young man who has a knee injury. After going to a physician for an X-ray and examination, he would care for his injured leg by wrapping it in an Ace bandage until healing occurred. This is a protective body barrier carried out on an overt, concrete level. Imagine again another young man who has a disability due to multiple sclerosis, muscular dystrophy, or other crippling disease. In this case, the disablement is neurological or muscular and a real Ace bandage would not be a concrete help. But what if the young man were to imagine his most vulnerable limbs wrapped in yards and yards of clean white gauze? Such creative visualization can provide support, comfort, and greater boundary definition. By consciously creating a more firm body-image barrier, one can cope more easily and rest more comfortably. Fear and anxiety are likely to diminish when you visualize a protective wrapping around yourself.

Many researchers who have followed in the footsteps of Fisher and Cleveland have found that people with high body-image barrier are able to cope more successfully with life's various challenges. In general, people with high body-image barrier have been found to behave more autonomously, show higher achievement motivation, and have better persistence in completing tasks than those with lower body-image barrier. They tend to have a strong sense of integrity and general personality strengths, and consequently they have better abilities to cope with many different kinds of challenges.

In addition to helping people to cope with physical injury and medical illness, the use of potent imaginal support for the body image can be invoked and strengthened whenever one has to cope with psychological as well as physical threat. When you feel anxious, one way to combat the feeling of being threatened is to mentally imagine a firm, secure barrier. If you visualize a shield, body armor, a protective cave, or yards of cotton batting to protect yourself, this imaginal shielding can provide a buffer against an angry assault or an intimidating encounter. Your efforts at assertiveness and your courage can be bolstered by this use of visual imagery to provide strength and support in frightening circumstances. In this way, you can allow yourself conscious control, using imagery to reinforce your defenses when needed. When you consciously erect such an imaginal defense, you can much more readily lay the image aside when your need for defense is past.

Visualization and Healing

New impetus in the use of visual imagery to aid healing arises in the work of such leaders as Lawrence LeShan, Bernie Siegel, and Stephanie and Carl Simonton. The visualization approach is not new, however. We know of historical evidence of the use of imagery in medicine dating back to the time of Aristotle, and the alchemists discovered that imagination is a tool that can be used to alter the material reality of the body. This work is corroborated by recent medical research that shows that imagery has direct effects on the physiology of your body. Jeanne Achterberg reports studies that have demonstrated: (1) ability to increase heart rate by imagining oneself running, (2) alteration of pupil size by imagining various sights, (3) dramatic physiological changes in male and female genitals accompanying sexual imagery, (4) changes in heart rate, muscle tension, and skin resistance that accompany the imagery of noxious stimuli, (5) measured changes in blood glucose, gastrointestinal activity, and blister formation dependent on varied uses of visual imagery, and (6) capability of the image to control several aspects of the immune system.

When you imagine a pleasant, nonthreatening scene, the physiological results in your body are lowered blood pressure, slowing of the heart, and a return to the homeostatic balance that keeps your body in a state of well-being. In contrast, if you call up intensive negative images (for example, recalling traumatic experiences from childhood) your heart will speed up and you will have increase in galvanic skin response, rapid breathing, and eye movements.

The recent experimental evidence of the effects of imagery on emotion and body functioning has convinced forward-thinking physicians to use psychological methods and to renew the ancient therapeutic use of visualization techniques. Leading surgeon Bernie Siegel describes a broad-based approach for treatment of cancer patients including relaxation, meditation, visualization, and hypnosis. As part of the treatment program, he encourages his patients to visualize their white blood cells and T-cells providing an active response to the invasive, out-of-control cancer cells. He claims that visualization takes advantage of a peculiar quirk in the human body, namely, that the body cannot distinguish between a vivid image and an actual physical experience.

The immune system responds to such therapeutic use of visual imagery. But sounding a note of caution against over-optimism, Siegel writes, "Unfortunately, this technique doesn't always work. We just don't know enough about the process.... From years of experience in using the visualization technique, however, we do know that the image must be chosen by the individual. It must be an image that that person can see in the mind's eye clearly.... It must be an image with which the patient feels completely comfortable."

Two common uses of visualization in medicine are, first, to imagine the immune system responding to the *cause* of the illness, and second, to use comforting images to soften and cope with *pain*. We can treat cancer pain in this manner. (Of course, this does not mean that we should fail to provide pain-killing medication as well.) Other pain, such as chronic muscle spasms or migraine, can also be an appropriate target for visualization techniques.

One patient had periodic lower back pain that recurred several times a year. At those times the pain worsened during her long car ride to work. She enjoyed swimming, which always made her back feel better. One day she spontaneously discovered that she could use the water imagery to lessen her pain while driving. Before starting her car, she sat in as relaxed a posture as possible. She began to visualize bubbles of water blowing around the area of her injured back muscles. Turquoise water and multitudes of bubbles felt free and soft. She found that she could make the water cool to help deaden the pain. She was able to keep up this imagery, with eyes open, as she started her car and began to drive. Halfway home, she found that she was imagining for others as well. She visualized cool turquoise bubbles for *all* people who suffer from back pain. Then, even more expansively, she found she was imagining the comforting bubbles for cancer patients and all who suffer any type of pain. In this expansive mood, she lost all awareness of her own pain. By using imagery in concern for others, she left behind the self-focus of her own discomfort.

In this case, there is a kinesthetic body response, as well as a visual component to the imaginal process. You can use any of the senses to augment the visual imagery. When your eyes are open, the visual imagination will naturally be less vivid than when you are in a meditative trance state with your eyes closed.

In contrast to these positive uses of imagination, we know that negative imagery arises in states of anxiety, and the negative images and thoughts frequently lead to the very dysfunction that we dread. When our aim is to cope gracefully, we must think positively and find positive uses of imagination to make it easier for us to accomplish our goals and achieve our desires. When we use imagery to combat everyday unhappiness, we gain the power to change the needless feelings of powerlessness and passivity that so often keep us lethargic. Those negative feelings often come about when we are self-critical and lead to apathy and loss of basic self-esteem. When we hold onto the images that relate to some type of loss, we usually fall into sadness, a sense of emptiness or void. Other troublesome feelings, such as anxiety, arise when we imagine some threatened or impending loss. I cannot overemphasize the fact that our feelings and actions occur in relation to what we *imagine* to be true about ourselves and our environment. One of the most fundamental principles in depth psychology is that our inner processes are channeled by what we anticipate. Both our actions and our feelings depend on what we imagine will occur in the future.

Imagery and Self-Hypnosis

So far, the imaginal techniques I have presented in this chapter are largely those that are under conscious control. We can *decide* to call up a positive image and to use a verbal affirmation to enhance daily life. There are additional deeper levels in the imaginal world that are only partially under our control. As we move to the deeper levels, you will begin to get some insight into trance and the hypnotic world.

Hypnosis draws heavily on the use of visual imagery to influence the unconscious mind. Milton H. Erikson was a creative genius who learned about the subtle relationship between images and the possibilities of growth while he taught himself to move and walk again after a childhood bout with polio. He developed his abilities and found that he could be an accurate observer and could spontaneously find images as a means to create change for himself and others. After he became a leading therapist, he described hypnosis as the communication of ideas to another person in such a way as to maximize his or her receptivity. The aim was to deeply motivate the person to find his or her own body potentials, thus leading to the control of psychological and physiological responses. The important point is that the patient does his or her own exploration of psychosomatic processes. The person under hypnotism is ultimately the one who finds the solution to the problem. The therapist serves as guide to help the person find entry into the unconscious realm so that she or he can identify and mobilize new resources for coping.

Many people have mixed reactions toward hypnotism. People who pride themselves on their conscious self-control may be particularly resistant to the idea of hypnotism. Of course, you are absolutely right to be wary of quackery and stage-hypnotism by untrained practitioners. However, hypnotism is a worthy technique with demonstrated usefulness in pain control and medicine. The use of hypnotism in pain control eliminates the need for excessive medication and may speed healing at the same time it is reducing discomfort. When used by competent practitioners, there is little danger of side effects from hypnotic trances.

As yet we cannot fully define the exact nature of trance and the hypnotic process. The most recent understanding is that hypnosis can be explained as an altered state of consciousness (ASC). This view borrows heavily from Eastern philosophy. William Kroger, co-founder of the American Society of Clinical Hypnosis and active in psychosomatic research, has expressed a firm view that all altered states of consciousness are related. In particular, the states induced by various types of meditative practice and relaxation techniques are similar. One thing they have in common is that they enhance internal awareness, resulting in greater preoccupation with internal sensations or mental processes. Physiological measures show us that there is a greater awareness of subtle sensory phenomena, coupled with almost complete elimination of motor activity. This gives a high sensory/motor ratio (S/M), which is common in all altered states.

Few people in the general population realize that there is a very close relationship between relaxation exercises, guided imagery, hypnotic trance, and meditative experience. It seems likely that these ASC form a continuum, ranging from very light trance to very deep, nearly mystical states. Nowadays it is becoming quite common to discover the use of guided imagery in many varied and ordinary circumstances. For example, you can find guided imagery and light trance being used in religious worship services, in preparation for sporting events, and in medicine. When guided imagery techniques are heavily interlaced with suggestion, these exercises might be considered forms of "deep persuasion." In my opinion, at their best, imagery techniques should be permissive and rely essentially on incorporating methods of "self-persuasion." Bernie Siegel's methods of visualization, which I described above, are examples of such widely useful, permissive methods of self-hypnotic suggestion.

An example of guided imagery that you can use for reducing anxiety and healing problems of self-esteem is given in Appendix A, Exercise 1, p. 191. Through imagery you establish trust when you choose a loving, trustworthy wisdom figure to guide and respond to you. You maintain trust throughout the exercise by the gentle, accepting attitude that you develop and use. You give and receive trust. The atmosphere is safe. This type of guided imagery acts as a very safe form of self-hypnosis. In this or other forms of hypnosis, the aim is to enter the unconscious for the purposes of dialog. We influence the unconscious by calling upon a positive, healing image. The result is lower anxiety, greater clarity and creativity in the problem areas of life. When you periodically use such gentle self-hypnotic methods, you will find that your sense of self-esteem gradually begins to improve.

Hypnosis is one form in which the dialog between conscious waking life and the unconscious mind can occur. Our ordinary waking lives are governed by consciousness and determined by the ego, that part of ourselves that likes to stay in control. On the other hand, we know the unconscious is rich in the resources of the deep underground stream. These resources are available to us through the use of imagery. It can be extremely potent and therapeutic to foster the dialog between the conscious and unconscious aspects of our minds. In hypnosis, the therapeutic goal is for a conscious will to influence the unconscious. Hypnosis is especially useful to alter habits, to provide anesthesia for pain, and/or to recover repressed memories. Yet another way in which the dialog between the conscious and the unconscious domains can be fostered is through dream work.

Dreams as the Window to the Unconscious

In working with dreams, we seek not so much to influence the inner mind as to learn from it. All dream work is based on the assumption that there is wisdom inherent in the unconscious that can be beneficial, if made conscious, for the welfare of the whole person. Consider the contrasting characteristics. The world of the unconscious is by nature imagistic and metaphorical, rather than verbal and concrete. The familiar world of the conscious is known for its qualities of awareness and willfulness. The conscious psyche is well adapted for dealing with the visible, active, and material aspects of the world. The unconscious, on the other hand, seems ambiguous as it synthesizes and creates wholes, often combining opposing things without being contradictory. Time and space in the realm of the unconscious are not linear, but multidimensional. Different moments can coexist in ways that are not possible in ordinary linear time. The unconscious does not adhere to our ways of understanding cause and effect. Rather, it moves by other laws of context and simultaneity.

In learning to comprehend the language of the unconscious, we need to be aware of the rich symbolic meanings behind metaphor and image. We also need to recognize the ways in which things operate differently than we would expect. Time and space differences collapse so that in dreams things can occur simultaneously when, in waking reality, we might expect them to be separated by many years or by great geographic distance. When this happens the unconscious is noting a similarity between "then" and "now." The people who inhabit our dreams may also merge into condensed images. We sometimes sense, for example, that the same person can be "both Aunt Susan and my best friend." One of the ways in which the unconscious can creatively communicate its message is by this efficient method of condensation. Such a blended image makes one wonder: What do Aunt

Susan and my best friend have in common? What could this double image symbolize?

We also know that waking life and dream life may compensate for one another. Jung thought that the compensatory function of the unconscious was extremely important. For example, when we are consciously puffed up with our own importance, that is, overinflated, dreams of falling often serve to keep the inner balance by bringing us back to earth. On the other hand, when we are feeling dejected, the unconscious often produces its most beautiful, affirming dreams so that our spirits are uplifted.

The unconscious also seeks to provide us with messages that we may need to correct our course in life. Learning to hear and heed the messages of the unconscious is very useful in coping with our everyday challenges. The seemingly mysterious dreamworld is not really in stark contrast or opposition to the objective day world. Rather, *both* waking consciousness and experiences in dreams are components of a potential unity based on cooperation within the psyche. Finding this unity is what Jung called the path of *individuation*. Amid the flux of change in our daily lives, we begin to individuate, finding our own unique ways to actualize our potentials in whatever manner the limits of our fate allow.

By way of introduction to working with dreams, I will first outline some points that I pass on to clients when we begin to explore their dreams in therapy; then I will give an example of a dream series with some suggestion of various messages that can be obtained from these pieces of unconscious material; and third, I will discuss some of the ways in which you can use "amplification," "active imagination," and "retaining the image" in conscious awareness.

Preparation and Beginning Dreamwork. The following suggestions have been helpful for people who are interested in beginning dream work but who may have some doubts about their ability to capture any dream material for study. First, you must recognize that we all dream. On the average, we dream about five times each night at roughly ninety-minute intervals. We have greater frequency and longer duration of dreams as we approach morning and time for awakening. You take the first most important step in dream work when you simply decide that you are really interested in your dreams and wish to recall them. Then you need to decide what method you will use to record your dream. If you sleep alone, a tape recorder can be useful. Otherwise, you will need to keep a dream journal and pen by your bedside. It is important to have what you need within reach so that you can record your dream before you have to become fully aroused. Before going to sleep, focus your attention on your desire to remember and understand your dreams. When you invite the dream, you begin the cooperative teamwork with your unconscious mind. Now if you awaken during the night with a dream memory, jot down a few key phrases. Even a few words may often be sufficient to stimulate your full recall in the morning. Remember that a dream left uninterpreted, that is, without any attempt at understanding, is like a letter unopened. When you begin to make consistent efforts to understand your dreams, they will reward you and you will quickly come to appreciate these valuable messages from the unconscious.

Next, it is helpful to let your waking imagination immerse itself in the dream images and to reexperience the scenes as they occurred in the dreams. The following suggestions and assumptions serve as guidelines:

• *After writing the dream down, use the imagery* to come to an intuitive understanding of the dream.

• *Work with the part of the dream that strikes you most.* Think about it and see what comes to mind about it. Just let your mind wander off. Don't try to make sense out of it. Dreams speak a language all their own and are not logical at all. It sometimes helps to draw or paint it, or to act out the dream either physically, as in role play, or in your imagination. You can also write a dialog in your journal with any of the characters in your dreams. Journal dialogs are frequently helpful in understanding the way a specific character symbolizes some aspect of your inner life.

• *Listen to the feelings* that are present in the dream or when you awake. Are there any areas in your life where that same feeling is present right now? Feelings often provide important clues to the dream as they are the major link between conscious and unconscious ways of knowing.

• *Watch and feel the energy* in your dream. Where is it leading? Where does it suggest you need to go?

• *Usually all parts of a dream are connected* in some way. And all aspects relate to some aspect of yourself. The dream shows what is going on in your inner life; and often it points the way for you to move ahead. A dream is a spontaneous message from the unconscious, and it is totally honest. Often the end of the dream suggests important directions for you to take.

• *Recognize the important symbols* in your dreams. These come out of your own inner life. Each one is unique, although it may also be connected to the "collective unconscious" of all humanity. Your dream comes from the depths of your soul. It is important not to presume that "this always means that." The translation is much more subtle and personal. Each dream symbol belongs to *you*. Treasure and value it. It is a gift you have been given.

Working with a Dream. In general, we use four major steps in the Jungian approach to dream interpretation: First, begin with a clear understanding of the exact details of the dream. Second, gather associations to the dream symbols. What comes to mind when you picture the particular image that appeared in the dream? Third, move on to wider amplifications, wondering, for example, how this image may have been expressed in other cultures and other periods of history. This is what Jung called the "archetypal" level of dream symbolism. Fourth, notice how the fully amplified dream relates to the context of your waking life. How is the dream serving in your process of individuation?

The following dream series will illustrate the ways in which the unconscious can help a person to make important decisions and to guide his or her life. Emily was fifty-two years old when she came into therapy. She looked drained and gaunt and very anxious as she sat slumped over. She was preparing for divorce because her husband was an alcoholic, with increasingly heavy drinking. He was also a womanizer. Although he often flirted, he had only once before been involved in an affair. Since he had retired two years ago, he had become involved with the widow in the condominium next door. The affair was blatant and quite painful for his wife. Emily herself was a recovered alcoholic with over twenty years membership in AA and a consistently "clean" record with never an alcoholic slip. She was a strong, shy, taciturn person who was always family-centered. She had been a secretary before having her three children but had no desire to return to work. Her husband had been a successful business executive, so money was not a problem at this stage of their life. When she entered therapy, she was painfully tense, particularly suffering from tightness and pain in her chest. While she was struggling to decide whether to pursue the divorce, she had a series of dreams. In the first, she recounted:

I stood on a bridge. As I looked into the water below, I saw numerous submarines floating by. As I looked more intently, I saw that one of these partially submerged objects was not a submarine but a large turd. Watching it, I thought, "That's a live one!"

This was the first dream of therapy. Her immediate association to the turd was that it was like her marriage: "a great big piece of shit" but also "a live one." Her feeling in the dream was predominantly surprise and relief. The marriage was not dead. There were many things that she disliked about it, many things that she felt were "dirty and smelly."

After discussing her personal associations and feelings about the dream, we talked also about the more universal, or archetypal, symbolism. In the dream, she was standing on a bridge. She was in fact in the middle of the bridge, not sure which shore she would approach. As she waited to make her decision, she looked into the water. She did not know it at the time, but water is a universal symbol of the unconscious. Submarines that travel underwater, like fish, are symbolic of unconscious contents that can come to the surface and be seen. The turd, of course, was her own personal symbol that dramatically expressed her feelings about her marriage.

The next week when she came for therapy, this woman reported that the pain in her chest was gone. She was still undecided about whether to pursue the divorce, but she wanted to work on ways to see if the marriage could be improved. Over the next several months she worked on assertiveness, on discovering her own desires and becoming less submissive. She also felt more free to spend time and money on her appearance, and she began to look much more attractive. She relaxed somewhat so her face looked less pained. Several dreams gave support to her efforts to find meaningful activities for herself. One bathroom dream suggested that she was, in fact, beginning to flush away the waste. While her husband continued to drink sporadically, at Emily's insistence, he extracted himself from the extramarital affair.

It was after about a year of therapy that another dream emerged. She reported it with a sense of awe. Although she had no comprehension of its meaning, she felt that this dream had real significance for her:

There was an island — a round island — with a huge tree on it. The roots of the tree grew down deep into the soil of the island. Next I saw an airplane coming in to land. It nearly hit the tree but managed to just brush by, landing safely, without harming the tree.

The people got off the plane. Many people walked off together in the same direction. Then my husband and I got off the plane. We walked away in a different direction.... Our direction was different from the rest of the crowd. Just as I awoke, I heard a word spoken. It was "Kismet."

As I listened to this dream, I too felt a sense of awe. We both knew that this was a "big dream." There was a feeling of sacredness, although we did not as yet know why. Immediately I knew that this feeling of awe is what Jung described as the "numinous," that is, highly positive energy that can carry almost mystical feeling. This is the feeling that comes with the appearance of images of the truest Self. The importance of this kind of dream is well described by James Hall in his book *Jungian Dream Interpretation,* where he writes, "Numinous experiences occur in some dreams and seem capable, if assimilated, of producing deep and lasting alterations in the personality structure, an effect parallel to some religious conversions and to some peak experiences in waking life."

Emily, still taciturn, had very few personal thoughts about this dream. She said, "Well, one thing is clear: We don't go the way of the rest of the crowd." She also wondered aloud what "Kismet" could mean, but had no idea beyond recognition of it as being the name of a Broadway play. I knew that the sense of "safe landing" of the aircraft suggests a good prognosis for the dreamer. There had been a danger — the tree was almost clipped — but this disaster was averted and the aircraft, which carried both the dreamer and her husband, landed safely.

In looking at the symbolism of the tree deeply rooted in the round island, we moved to the archetypal level of dream amplification. In Jung's comprehensive research on cross-cultural symbolism, he found in myth and ritual as well as dreams that archetypes emerge as powerful, universal themes. These archetypes can and do occur for all of us. Jung found, for example, that the great tree often symbolizes the centering of the Self. It is the *axis mundi* or world tree. The great tree can also represent the Great Mother, a god-symbol, or the most central core of the dreamer's personality. Here the Great Tree was in danger. Something very sacred could have been damaged. But the danger was averted. We noticed that this tree is very deeply rooted. It could not easily be blown away. This reflects the strength of the dreamer's personality. She was an earthy woman who would not easily be uprooted.

As the plane lands, the crowd, the collective mass of ordinary people, all go off in one direction. The dreamer and her spouse go a different way. Their route is not the usual way. As they do leave, the word is spoken. "Kismet." What does it mean? We ended our session that night with the mystery unresolved. I gave her the assignment to see what she could learn about that mysterious word. I thought she would go to the library to see whether she could learn anything from the plot of the play by that name. Meanwhile, I turned to my dictionary. By the next day, we had both found the answer to the fascinating mystery. She called me in glee: "Kismet" means "fate"! We both laughed in recognition of how well that tied together the meaning of the whole dream. It is delightful to see how creative the unconscious can be. As so often happens, a single word provided the clue that helped Emily to grasp the personal meaning of the entire dream.

The excitement of unraveling a dream is heightened when mysterious pieces fall together and the whole puzzle is revealed. After this experience, the dreamer knew in the deepest recesses of her heart that this was her fate. Her suffering in life included alcoholism and an infidelity with which she had to cope. She would not divorce her husband. In the dream, Emily and her husband went off in a different direction than the rest of the crowd. Their fate is different from what most others would do. Even though half of the marriages end in divorce; even though most women might divorce a man who is alcoholic and having an affair, in spite of all that, this dreamer knew, as a gift from the unconscious inner source of her own wisdom, that for *her* the path was different. The marriage was alive; she would stay with her husband. She knew intuitively this decision was right. She knew it in the core of her being. She would go on and find ways to continue her search for enrichment in life. Divorce was not a path she needed to take. She felt happy and relieved. The decision had been made. Her dreams had affirmed that, for *her*, this choice was absolutely right.

This dream is an important one for the dreamer in many ways. One clue to its significance is the appearance of what Jungians describe as a symbol of the Self. As James Hall writes:

> The Self is the regulatory center of the entire psyche, while the ego is only the center of personal consciousness. . . . The Self often

takes the form of a symbol of higher value: images of God, the sun as the center of the solar system, the nucleus as the center of the atom, etc. The affective tone of an experience of the Self is often numinous or fascinating and inspiring of awe.... The Self may appear as a reassuring symbol of order, often in the form of a mandala.

The Great Tree is a common symbol of Self in the dreams of people who are in the process of individuation, usually at midlife or beyond. There are many other such symbols. These include images that emphasize a central element with symmetry around it. A feeling of awe and positive energy that accompanies these mandala images is often the easiest way to recognize the appearance of symbols of the Self archetype.

Carrying the Dream Image Onward. Reference in dreams to archaic rituals, ancient art objects, or international themes often suggests the appearance of archetypal elements that are emerging. In many cases, the sense of mystery is present and may not be easily resolved. When we interpret dreams, it is important never to feel that the dream has been exhausted. We can often find a useful, current meaning to the dream. In the light of subsequent dreams and events, the meaning may shift and we should expect modification of understanding as we go along. Dream interpretation involves a *continuing* dialog between the waking conscious mind and the unconscious.

Those of us who spend time with dreams often become delightfully immersed in the imagery. When you pay conscious attention to this dream world with its metaphorical language, you can gradually learn to comprehend its messages. One method for extending the inner dialog between conscious and unconscious is through the method that Jung called *amplification.*

In order to amplify our understanding of a symbol, we move to the archetypal level, searching for cross-cultural meanings. For example, if a dream lion appears, we search out every possible manifestation of "Lion." Power, strength, ferocity are the immediate associations; also the stealthy behavior of a cat and its impressive autonomy. Considering myths in which the lion appears, and its modern appearance in the Wizard of Oz and the MGM film logo, can further our understanding and deepen our appreciation of the meaning of the symbol. A trip through an art museum will yield many more images to nourish the ways in which we perceive "Lion." Royal heraldry and designations such as "lionhearted" are based on this archetype of strength. The lion image speaks of majesty and courage. It may appear in dreams at the very time that these qualities are most needed by the person who must cope.

Jung was truly a master of the art of amplification. He could take a symbol and trace it through numerous cultures, throughout the ages. His broad cultural knowledge allowed him to make easy associations and connections between the image and the meaning. He emphasized the need to stick to the image rather than trying to fit the image to a preconceived theory. In *The Development of Personality*, Jung wrote:

> Interpretation must guard against making use of any other view-points than those manifestly given by the content itself. If some-one dreams of a lion, the correct interpretation can lie only in the direction of the lion; in other words, it will be essentially an *amplification* of this image. Anything else would be an inad-equate and incorrect interpretation, since the image "lion" is a quite unmistakable and sufficiently positive presentation.

In addition to amplification, in which we research the dream image for its cross-cultural manifestations, we can also pursue the personal meaning of the image through *active imagination*. In this way, we take the image back inside and, with the conscious mind, we try it on for size. We ask: In what way does this image relate to me? In what ways is there "lion" in me? Is this a strength I need right now to cope with my challenges in life?

Almost invariably an image appears in a dream because it represents an unrecognized or undervalued part or attitude of the person who is dreaming. This subjective interpretation is an essential aspect of learn-ing from the wisdom of dreams. The symbols we encounter represent unknown aspects of ourselves. They are waiting for us to acknowledge them and invite them into integration with our conscious understand-ing of ourselves. We can never fully grasp the symbol in terms of what we already know. The very nature of the symbol is to take us beyond. Working with dreams, therefore, expands our consciousness and makes us more fully aware of who we really are.

In this way, we expand our capacity to cope with our lives and the challenges we face. For example, a dream may indicate the need to be-come more assertive by picturing a friendly lion. One way to come in touch with some needed "lionliness" would be to go back in imagination to dialog with the dream image. Journaling can be a productive way to foster this dialog. You ask a question of the imaginary lion and then allow the lion to respond. In your writing, you can continue the dialog until you feel some resolution. Another way would entail acting out that image, for example, with the help of a mask to dance and roar the role of a lion until the lion presence becomes emotionally incorporated into your conscious life.

There are numerous ways in which we can learn to establish contact with imagery and to move into that realm. Visualization is one method that encourages creativity and activates healthy coping mechanisms. We know that when people are in difficult periods of their lives, it is to their advantage to confront the forces they fear. When you face a frightening dream image, you are actually confronting a force of fear that resides within you. In dream work and active imagination we try to discourage passivity and encourage active involvement with the images. The dream images symbolize inner forces and dynamics within your personality, so you can gain much self-knowledge and improve your coping capacity by venturing courageously into this inner world.

In her book *Waking Dreams*, Mary Watkins suggests several specific techniques that are useful for active imagination: First, the psyche seems to govern and offer you protection by providing *helpful guide figures* at times of transition, and you can respond to the direction they suggest. These figures might take various forms such as an animal, a good parental image, a god-image, a wise old person, or a beautiful, competent young person. These figures can often guide you through troublesome situations and show you how you need to grow.

Second, *confrontation* is an important strategy when you encounter dream images that threaten your safety. With threatening animals or frightening people, it is vital to confront rather than to struggle or try to escape. As you stand steady and observe, you can begin to notice every detail of the image. By staring at the threatening being, you become less afraid and you have an opportunity to discover the message this image is intending to bring in its emergence from the unconscious right now.

A third strategy of active imagination is to *nurture* the image. Either a frightening or a pathetic image may suggest some inner aspect needing to be nurtured. You might cradle a malformed infant and give it milk until it grows, for example. In this way you can face the frightening and/or lonely aspects of your psyche by giving them due recognition and allowing them to be transformed.

Often when you confront a frightening being or nourish a weakling, the image changes and its symbolic message becomes easier to comprehend. The result of successful active imagination is that your personality will ultimately become stronger and more integrated. Optimally, you aim to incorporate the images that emerge in a new and more expansive inner peace. Gradually, you will begin to realize that when you turn away from aspects of yourself, or when you see them only as things to be overcome, they tend to become cut off from your conscious awareness. In that cutoff state, they become troublesome. This is a very important point. What you try to keep unconscious is what threatens you from the inner world. Befriending the images is a powerful and therapeutic way to overcome conflicts and to move toward inner peace. Thus the fourth strategy is *reconciliation*. With an unknown figure, for example, or with an image of a known person who is not actually present in your waking life, you can be friendly, show tenderness, and communicate positively. When you imagine a dialog between forces in your personality, you will find this to be a very therapeutic method for resolving inner conflicts. Often it is effective to begin this dialog in your dream journal, as soon as you have completed writing the dream.

These methods for the use of active imagination encourage creative ways to incorporate dream imagery into waking consciousness. The mental imagery that arises should be absolutely spontaneous, however. This is a vital point. The difference between surface level use of imagination and accessing the deeper level is a difference in conscious control. When you surrender control, the deeper imagery that arises spontaneously is a much more powerful connection with the unconscious psyche. When an image arises without any preplanning, you can honor its validity as a message from the unconscious Self. This spontaneous imagery can be truly liberating. Blockages and resistances to growth are resolved as you encounter the dream images, carrying them forward in active, imaginal ways.

A final way in which you can carry the dream image onward is through memory and *recollection*. Since not all dream images can be immediately interpreted, you often have the opportunity to mull over a mysterious dream and wonder about it for a period of time. When you rest with an image, bringing it to mind from time to time, you incorporate its power, even though you may not consciously understand it. The image itself, when you attend to it and bring it to your conscious awareness, works a process of transformation. Mary Watkins expresses this point very beautifully when she writes: "The psyche reveals herself in the form of images, for that is her experience. If we wish to befriend her, to love her, we must take great care in how we react to her, as her life speaks of itself to us. Our relation to the image, therefore, becomes all important." To learn of the imaginal world, you need to rest with the images that you have received. You need to put theory and assumptions aside and return again and again to the image. Each time you will experience it anew. Gradually, you will be able to see for yourself the specific meaning of this symbol in its specific time and place. In its own way, at its own pace, the symbol touches your awareness and its meaning unfolds.

Dreams as Answers to Personal Challenges. As we incorporate dreams' metaphoric wisdom into waking life, we come to more thorough self-knowledge and transformation of personality. As this inner wisdom emerges, our personal potentials unfold. Montague Ullman, founder of the Maimonides Dream Laboratory and expert in dream interpretation, emphasizes the potential that dreams have both to promote personality growth and to cope with ongoing, everyday challenges. He writes of our need for dreams in order to cope with the complexities of living. In the midst of our varied everyday challenges, dreams help us to define our existence and to discover the unique individual self we have it in us to be.

Ullman and his colleague, Nan Zimmerman, have written a delightful book entitled *Working with Dreams.* In response to the question of whether dreams solve problems, these authors say, "If the issue is one which genuinely concerns us and if, somewhere in our past experience, we had the resources needed to deal with it, we can, in our dreams, discover those resources and restructure them to highlight their bearing on a current problem." In this way we see that dreams can be very practical. Not only are they fascinating and uniquely personal, but they also have survival value.

We sleep to rest our bodies, and we dream to incorporate our daily experiences into the storehouse of memory. Our personal history is full of emotional richness, and each new day is full of experiences that must be integrated into what we already know and into the storehouse of our feelings about past events. When a challenge arises, the unconscious

mind functions during sleep to dip into the storehouse of "similar circumstances" in order to expose unrecognized aspects of past strengths
and vulnerabilities. Dreams pull forth information from past experience
that will contribute to the solution of present problems. Dreams also
pull forth both resources and defenses that may be needed to cope
with the current situation.

A great deal of this process remains in the unconscious, since the
vast majority of our dreams are never recalled. When we do remember
a dream, however, it is certainly valid to ask what bearing it might have
on our current conflicts and decisions. A dreamer in therapy had been
separated from his wife for two years. He was preparing to pursue formal divorce proceedings, but he was not absolutely sure that he should
proceed with that action. For about a week, he began to imagine what
it would be like to return to his wife and children. He felt nostalgic
and recalled past times when there had been love at home. During this
time of reconsidering, he had a dream:

> There was a house that my wife and I were trying to refurbish. But it
> was an impossible task. The house was black and charred. The floor
> was a gaping hole and the roof leaked from numerous places.

The dreamer quickly recognized the house symbolized his marriage.
Once the house was happy but that was a stage in his life that could
not be recaptured. The old house was beyond repair now. The marriage
could not be salvaged. No rebuilding efforts would be sufficient. He
decided to go ahead with the divorce.

Major life decisions should never be made impulsively. The old saying that suggests we "sleep on it" allows the unconscious to contribute
to our decision-making process. When we allow our lives to unfold in
a natural way, we can include the input of the vast wisdom housed
in our unconscious minds. Our natural creative resources are available
on a nightly basis. Through dreams we tap into the creative flow of the
underground stream.

Creativity

When we think of the underground river as the deep flow of the
psyche, we recognize a commonality to our human experience. The
underground river feeds the unconscious wellsprings of all of our souls.
Many people still fear this unknown realm; the fear itself is universal.

Each of us is a child of longing; each of us, at some deep level, yearns for love. None of us has been so privileged in childhood that we did not know moments of loneliness, times when we feared abandonment. Out of those early, preverbal fears of rejection and feelings of desolation flows our yearning to be loved. That in itself is common to the human condition. The underground river of human suffering unites us in longing for love. It unites us in empathy and compassion for one another. It flows through suffering and longing to places of rich and fertile creativity. When we look deep into our inmost soul, we come to compassion and healing. The waters of the underground river know both suffering and immense abiding joy. We must journey through the suffering to find the deeper joys. Out of our longing for love and beauty, the creativity of all humanity arises.

When we go inward in our search for internal, emotion-focused coping, we tap down into the wellspring of creativity. Out of our pain and sorrow, we reach for answers that transcend the ordinary. Out of desperation with the frustrations of "the way things are," we reach for new beginnings, new possibilities, new ways of comprehending reality.

All creativity arises out of the deep unconscious, the underground stream. Creativity is for everyone. Time out for appreciation of the arts enhances our lives and fosters positive emotional adaptation and coping. For those who produce creative works, the benefit is most significant. But the gift of creative products allows others to enjoy the arts as well. Appreciation of the arts lifts us. Emotional uplift is natural both when we participate and when we appreciate the aesthetic process. We see and understand beauty in many ways. Music, art, drama, dance, and humor all relate to emotion-focused coping. We sense beauty in the form, the synthesis, the transcendence, the energy, the definite structure and the meaning that a work of art conveys. We can enjoy each of the creative arts in its own seemingly magical context. All the arts uplift our spirits and allow us to improve our human sensitivity. I immediately recall how *wonderful* it felt when a friend sent me a beautiful bouquet of flowers when I was in the midst of the stressful process of cleaning out my house after the fire. One small space of beauty allowed me to cope with the soot and mess everywhere else. In this way art promotes our feeling of well-being. The underground stream flows richly, and emotion-focused coping is enhanced.

In essence, is life an expression of vast cosmic humor? Is life a dance? A tapestry? A symphony? Or a poem? Art expresses life, and art is a metaphor for life as we know it. Life is a mystery — a multifaceted jewel. We see first one side and then another. See now your strength, your autonomy, your liberty. Turn again and see your limitations, your dependence, your inevitable death. How can we cope with that? As we grapple with these contradictions and attempt to live out our fate with grace and courage, it helps immeasurably to recognize the creative resources that lie deep within the psyche. Each of us has a wellspring that taps the underground river. Each of us is creative, and we mold our lives in a uniquely personal way. To cope gracefully with the difficult challenges that life sends is to utilize our resources creatively.

Life is transitory. It occupies a very short span of time, like a piece of music or of dance. As we each look back on the life we have lived so far, we see both dark and light. Listening to the music of our lives over time, we hear both high notes, thrilling in exultation, and low notes, deeply resonant with sorrow and pain. At times of suffering, illness or frustration, it helps to remember that life is not always as it is at this moment. It helps immeasurably to view life from a broad cosmic perspective.

The gentle humor and creative support of life teach us to let go of our self-importance, our illusions, and our insistence on absolutes. Instead we begin to discover around us a fragile ambiguity that calls us to diminish the importance of our everyday life without ceasing to love it. Each small creative bit of life is a spark of the greater creativity of the universe.

In coping with the difficult challenges that life sends us, we need to use the creative spark within us. We can find inspiration and emotional uplift when we observe and participate in the arts. The arts serve to attune us to nature and help us recognize the inner harmony that gives us peace.

Alan Watts once observed that liberation consists of finding an erotic relationship with our surrounding environment — a loving, playful intimacy with every aspect of the world around. To be in love with the world, in love with life, enhances the aesthetic sensitivity in each of us. It is the artist in us, that mystical creative wisdom, that can see intuitively and appreciate deeply the vast panorama of life itself, the shadows and darkness as well as the light.

3

Good Relationships
Smooth the Way

THE SECOND STREAM contributing to the Tao of coping is the "Way of Social Support." This stream applies to all those coping methods we use to harmonize our emotions by reaching out to people in the external environment for their support and encouragement. We venture out in relation to others, knowing that we can grow and learn from each person we meet. When we keep open to the unexpected, we shape a new and more vibrant way of living.

Psychologists who have studied adult development throughout the life span emphasize the importance of building and maintaining a healthy support network that provides life satisfaction and a sense of well-being. Harvard researcher George Valliant did a long-term study on healthy psychological development and concluded that the most significant factor is the *quality of sustained relationships*. He found that mental health in adulthood depends less on early childhood trauma than we previously thought. Rather, mental health and well-being is most closely related to the presence of continuing, nurturing friendships. Without support communities where close friendships are vibrant, many nuclear couples and single individuals feel overburdened and are often isolated. In our vast, impersonal, bureaucratized society, people too often feel cut off from real social interaction. Then they feel alone, even bereft, as they try to meet the emotional and practical demands of daily living. Good relationships are especially important to cultivate in middle age as a bulwark against excessive loneliness in old age. Too many of us tend to become isolated when old friends begin to die or to move away.

Psychologist Peggy Thoits has explored the many ways in which social support acts as a buffer to protect people against the negative effects of major life stresses. We know that such normal life transitions as the empty nest syndrome, bereavement, and retirement are stressful; and some of us face added trials such as divorce, job loss, accidents, or serious illness. At such times, we need social support to buffer us, allowing us to cope with life more adaptively. Social support bolsters our self-esteem as it helps us modify our emotional reactions to the difficulties we face. For a person in need, it provides a sense of group belonging. Another way social support strengthens us to cope with troublesome emotions is by helping us to find a sense of meaning or purpose when circumstances require major life changes.

Not all social support is effective, however. The quality of the relationship matters tremendously. People naturally seek out relationships where they feel accepted. A helper must be emotionally attuned and empathic to be effective. She or he must be able to express love or caring and respect. In general, those relationships which provide acceptance, hope, joy, and love are likely to be sustaining and helpful. In contrast, in those relationships where anxiety, depression, and anger predominate, those negative emotions (called the "unholy trio") may breed on one another and fester chronically.

Any human life is full of difficulties, conflicts, and frustrations. It is normal to experience the whole range of positive and negative emotions every day of your life. Even in crises, emotions flow naturally when you feel them, pass through them, and let them go. Being aware of your feelings is the key to being able to move from one emotion to another, so you remain alive and unstuck. Psychotherapists know the miracle of healing that occurs when one is able to get deeply in touch with the more painful emotions and then to let go. Feeling and letting go of the deeper pain allows the lighter emotions to surge in, resulting in a feeling of freedom and attunement.

Meaningful relationships allow you to release negative emotions so that feelings of acceptance and hope can return and produce their healing effects. Ordinarily, depression is troublesome only when you dwell excessively on losses from the past; and anxiety is a generalized fear about the future. If even one supportive person can bring love into a tragic situation, there is less despair. A friend who provides laughter also lifts the heart with joy. When someone close communicates genuine hope, it brings the sense that there is something worth living for in the future. In this way, hope, love, and joy counteract the darker emotions. Social support also helps to buffer your present sense of self-esteem and belonging so that you can cope more easily with the feelings of loss, frustration, or anxiety about the future.

In this chapter, I will discuss several different kinds of relatedness that can be supportive and nourishing. We will look first at friendships in which mutuality and respectful interdependence are the key elements. Second, we will explore the experience of "being in love" with its abundant energies. Third, we will think about recurrent patterns in family systems with some thoughts on co-dependence. Finally, we will look at support networks and communities, which are very helpful in relieving feelings of loneliness.

Friendship

Loneliness and lack of companionship are among the greatest unrecognized contributors to illness and premature death. Recent research shows the immune system is adversely affected by loneliness, so we are becoming increasingly aware that long, healthy lives are more likely for people who have good interpersonal relationships. In order to strengthen the bonds with others and to have a full and rewarding social life, we need to reach out, to open ourselves so that we can touch and be touched by others. To be truly available for deep intimate relationships, we need to accept our personal limitations. We need to be willing to lower our masks and allow more of our true selves to appear to the other. When we acknowledge and accept our vulnerability as human beings, we become more willing to expose ourselves, both our strengths and weaknesses. Trust is built by mutual sharing of our authentic selves.

To have a truly intimate friendship, we must risk mutual revelation. We reveal ourselves most effectively when we do so gradually. It requires faith in each of us to give the self to another. We are motivated by the desire to reach beyond our individual selves. As we are open and risk exposing ourselves to one another, we become less inhibited. We develop the ability to express ourselves both verbally and nonverbally. With practice and commitment, our methods of communication can improve. Shyness, inhibition, and fear that the other will not accept the truth about who we are will fade as we grow in trust and mutual self-revelation. Inevitably our personality, including our imperfections, will show. In real friendship, as we grow in awareness of our human-ness we experience also an intimacy and a deepening awareness of the other as a whole and real person.

The number of friends we have and how long those relationships thrive may be affected by proximity and by shared interests, but clearly, all good relationships require effort. To be true friends, we need to be able to depend on one another. We care and are generously concerned for each other. Even when time, energy, or other resources are scarce or when we are separated by many miles, as friends we have an abiding sense of our mutual affection. Authentic relationships are never one-sided. Mutuality means that each of us can count on the affection, acceptance, and enduring good will of the other. We have an unspoken pact that our friendship matters to each of us.

Throughout life, friendship is an essential ingredient to vibrant liv-ing. As we grow older, our personalities become more highly developed and we often find that our capacity for deep, mutually rewarding rela-tionships increases. The rich tapestry of life is open for friends to share together.

Intimate Relationships

What is it that creates a *special* relationship? The closest anyone can come to defining love is a poetic description of falling in love. The experience is undescribable, ineffable, unfathomable. Yet in that ex-perience, you find a mystery with such palpable energy that you can perceive it vividly. Often you may need to channel and direct the flow of loving energy. Freud defined "libido" as the sexual attraction that, in the fullness of its expression, unites two human beings in lov-ing genital union. For a time, there may be a blending, not only of bodies, but also of heart, mind, and spirit. Yet this confluence, this total coming together, is never complete. Though we often yearn to feel total safety, security, and being loved, nonetheless union may be fleeting. A sense of confluence waxes and wanes with the tides of emo-tional life and the changing needs of the partners. Yet desire for this full expression of loving energy is as powerful as any psychic energy on earth.

Desire for union with a beloved partner is far more than physio-logical. The physical aspects of this drive create arousal, which we experience as deliciously energizing. Many a sleepless night has been spent by a lover longing for his or her partner. The flowering of that de-licious desire is psychological, as well as physiological. Mind and body unite in their yearning for oneness with the other. The desire for a *soul mate* pervades and infuses all our thoughts, all our plans, all our ac-tions. Imagery and fantasy of the presence of the lover fill the hours and warm our waiting hearts. Being "head over heels in love" is an apt metaphor. Life indeed seems to be turned upside down. Plans, aims, goals may all be set spinning as the desire for relationship with the beloved takes precedence, guiding our choices, setting our priorities, claiming our attention.

Many artists have been inspired to produce great works by this in-tense erotic energy. On the other hand, men have fought wars and kingdoms have fallen when the energy of erotic desire has become en-tangled with self-serving power drives. On a smaller scale, when erotic energy is diverted into an extramarital affair, there is also the risk of destroying the family bonds of one or both of the lovers. So we see that libido can be creative and beneficial, or it can be destructive, for individuals, for families, or for society at large. It all depends on how you use it. When you become involved and risk yourself in a relation-ship, you must decide whether your erotic energies will find their flow in creative, rather than hurtful, processes. When you and your part-ner are able to love as mature human beings, you are open to joining expressively in your mutual attraction. In this, you become open and vulnerable enough to share both your talents and gifts as well as your desires, hopes, and needs.

As lovers, not only do you celebrate your mutual desire and close-ness but also, in the ebb and flow of life, you must be able to withstand the separations. You must be strong enough to stand alone. Each member of a healthy partnership must work toward being "differen-tiated." By this I mean that each of us must be an individual, first and always. No matter how close and intimate a relationship becomes, you must never sacrifice your unique individuality. You are together but you are also ultimately different, too. As Kahlil Gibran writes in *The Prophet* of the intimate relationship: "Let there be spaces in your togetherness.... Love one another, but make not a bond of love... stand together yet not too near together: For... the oak tree and the cypress grow not in each other's shadow."

When Love Is Mixed with Other Needs

There are many ways in which relationships can go awry. Most adults have suffered, at one time or another, from heartbreak when what once seemed an idyllic love affair ended in break-up. For some people, however, heartbreak seems to be a repetitive, endless state of affairs. Some people are so prone to having chaotic relationships that they live in a chronic state of distress. One such person, I'll call Pam, came to therapy because of sexual dysfunction. At first, she was very nervous and cried when she said that she was unable to have satisfying intercourse. After she started to relax, she gradually came to realize the importance of expressing her own desires. It took many months of psychotherapy before she was able to recognize that she, too, had a right to a gratifying sexual experience.

Pam had a big heart and strong tendencies to play the martyr role. She was devoted to working for good causes. Her identity was deeply connected with her sense of service to the poor and social action aimed against injustice. Deeply imbedded in her personality structure, Pam suffered from an unconscious sense of guilt. She told me that her parents always seemed to want her to be something other than what she really was. They always taught her to give but never to receive. Pam learned to cope with this family situation by trying to rise above it. She tended to have a sense of moral superiority because of her efforts at self-sacrifice. While Pam productively applied her self-sacrificing attitude in genuine service for social causes, her difficulty in intimate relationships was the result of her underlying guilt. She deeply believed that she was unworthy to receive love and gratification. Because of this guilt, she was prone to establishing relationships with men who would abuse, exploit, or ignore her.

It was clear that Pam needed to learn that she herself was a worthwhile person; that she, like any other human being, had the right to the pursuit of happiness; and that, in her earnest efforts to care for all of humanity, she herself was worthy. In caring for others, she had forgotten to provide for her own care and attention. In therapy, her sexual responsiveness began to improve. Then progressively she found herself pursuing less destructive relationships. She began to understand that her self-sacrifice had been excessive and misguided. She had persistently chosen the wrong kind of men. Gradually she began to respect herself and to choose her partners more wisely.

All therapists know that there is a type of martyrdom where one gives too much. This comes from misunderstanding the fundamental religious message. For example, the Christian cross symbolizes the loving acceptance of suffering, but the idea of "turn the other cheek" can sometimes lead to misguided self-sacrifice and dysfunctional relationships. *Endurance is not meant to be a masochistic form of self-victimization.* Ironically, masochism or martyrdom tends to be self-righteous and is often unconsciously controlling. The masochist exercises control over others by being their victim.

I often tell people like Pam: "When you must bear suffering, do so only because you have no other viable alternative. You may in fact need to surrender, but if you must accept the hostility of others, you need to be clear about your motives and what you are giving up." This world is full of enough suffering without seeking opportunities to increase one's own discomfort. But this is exactly what many people do when they unconsciously set themselves up to fail, whether that failure is in work or in intimate relationships. Whenever you consistently set aside your own needs in a relationship and lay down your life for another, you risk falling into what I call "the doormat syndrome." If your love is mixed with guilt and masochism, it may require psychotherapy to help you work your way through to self-acceptance. It is essential to accept and care for yourself before you will be able to have genuine, mutually rewarding relationships.

We know that healthy sexual expression includes respect, concern, and caring for the whole social context of both the lovers. Relationships are healthy when trust and honest communication are central and when sexuality transcends self-gratification and performance. In fact, sexual pleasure is heightened in the context of *mutual* devotion. In treasuring the differences and tenderly caring for one another's vulnerabilities, lovers promote the genuine individuation of each.

Pursuit and Distance: The Old Two-step

When you set out upon the task of increasing your awareness and honing your skills in the art of relationship, it is good to realize that the potential for true intimacy often lies in playfulness rather than deadly seriousness. If you are going to play like a winner, it's a good idea to learn the way the game is played. Family therapist Phil Guerin tells us that stagnation is a total lack of playfulness, and it can happen in two ways. Stagnation occurs when what seems to be an absence of conflict is actually a screen masking a malignant form of emotional deadness and fusion. On the other hand, stagnation can also happen when a struggle has gone on too long and the conflict has become deadly and destructive. If you are caught in a stagnant relationship, sometimes you may be able to revitalize and renew it. The best ways are, first, by opening your communications with each other and, second, by learning about the repeated relationship patterns that occur between you and your partner. This learning gives you a fresh opportunity to replace the patterns that aren't working with other, more effective ways.

One pattern that occurs universally in two-person relationships is known among family systems experts as the pattern of pursuit and distance. Let's see how that works. People tend to behave in stereotypical, repetitive ways, and these tendencies may depend both on their cultural background and on the present context. In general, *pursuers* tend to value movement toward people. They move in emotionally, tending to value honesty and truth. Sometimes they move toward others without sufficient sensitivity, so that their statements are ineffective, blunt, or seemingly cruel. The pursuer enters relationships seeking togetherness, a sense of "we-ness," and a desire to share. If you are a pursuer, you may harbor hopes that you will somehow find completion when someone outside yourself fills you up. *Distancers*, on the other hand, tend to move away from emotional intensity. Distancers are often careful and protective of their own space. They may be indirect and vague, especially when threatened by emotionality that puzzles them. If you are a distancer, you may tend to want to pacify others. The distance you create is often a result of your attempts to find peace at any price.

In close relationships, when anxiety arises, pursuers renew their habits of moving in, wanting to talk problems out and to regain closeness. Meanwhile, distancers are busy seeking greater separation, preferring to handle their emotional turmoil in solitude. Each of the reciprocal patterns, pursuit and distance, becomes more pronounced when anxiety is high.

The roots of this process lie in the fact that all of us want *closeness*. We want to belong somewhere, to be cared about and accepted, even with our faults. Often we do not realize that we must work at being close. Closeness is fluctuating, here and then gone; it is not a constant state. Two people move toward each other, and the closer they get to loving one another, the greater are their expectations, their desire for completion, and their hope of fulfillment. From the pursuer's perspective, the aim is to avoid the feeling of nothingness inside; the tendency is to pursue in order to fill oneself from others. Otherwise the pursuer may feel habitually empty or even dead inside.

While one person becomes the emotional pursuer, such intensity may be overwhelming to the other, which leads to his or her reactive distance. If you are a distancer, you try to protect your space from the intrusion of the other. You distance to reestablish your aloneness. Sometimes this means you have to live with your loneliness. Whereas pursuers are addicted to seeking togetherness, distancers seek beauty from afar. From distance everything is soft and graceful, but this reserve may be a foretaste of loneliness.

None of us is entirely oriented toward one pattern or the other. The amount you tend to pursue or distance is relative. When you examine your feelings and behavior over a period of time, you begin to discover that you show both patterns in different situations, but you will also see which one predominates. Self-awareness will help you to choose the most effective movement, so you can respond consciously to the particular needs in your relationship at that moment.

When we add some playfulness and explore differing ways of being together, we keep the relationship lively. Then we are less likely to become stuck and uncomfortable. As family therapists warn: Never pursue a distancer! But they also know it will probably not be effective if you try to distance from a pursuer. I remember when my children were little, I needed to get some space and time alone for myself. I used to get up early and go outside in summer time for some peaceful gardening at 6:00 A.M. That worked just fine until my little three-year-old daughter discovered where I was. Then she began to come out every morning to talk to me. So much for peace and quiet. Never distance from a pursuer! (It doesn't work.) The best advice may simply be: If what you're doing isn't working, do something else! With perspective and some degree of humor, we can see these pursuit and distance movements as a dance in which each partner seeks a comfortable position. Back and forth we dance, males and females, pairs of all sorts, in the two-step together.

The See-Saw Effect

How we work together is another very important aspect of partnership. Every couple must work out their own balance and efficient way to handle the tasks they share. The way couples work together in marriage begins with courtship. When you choose a mate you are significantly influenced by both emotional and instinctual forces. For example, instincts affect our choices in that we tend to choose a partner who has approximately the same level of emotional maturity that we do. We unconsciously choose one another on the basis of the level of emotional health in the two families from which we have come. The greater the level of dysfunction in the families of origin, the greater the potential for problems in the future.

One way in which potential problems may become overt is in the dominance patterns of the relationship. Master family therapist Murray Bowen has stated the matter succinctly in Phil Guerin's book *Family Therapy*:

> One [partner] may assume the dominant role and force the other to be adaptive, or one may assume the adaptive role and force the other to be dominant. Both may try for the dominant role, which results in conflict; or both try for the adaptive role, which results in decision paralysis. The dominant one gains self at the expense of the more adaptive one.... The dominant and adaptive positions are *not* directly related to the sex of the spouse. They are determined by the position that each had in their families of origin. From my experience, there are as many dominant females as males and as many adaptive males as females. These characteristics played a major role in their original choice of each other as partners.

In any marriage, a fairly good degree of flexibility in terms of who takes the leadership is undoubtedly a good sign. Flexibility bodes well for the future. In less healthy families, we are likely to find chronic patterns of dominance in one partner with the other partner taking a more passive role. Chronic passivity and chronic dominance patterns are both likely to be maladaptive in the long run. The individual who functions for a long period of time in the passive position may gradually lose the ability to function well and make decisions for himself or herself. When one partner becomes "underfunctioning," the other chooses, or is forced into, the "overfunctioning" position. It works just like a see-saw. When one is in the "up" position in terms of taking responsibility, the other one is "down." What seems to work best is a fairly even balance of responsibility or, at worst, mild fluctuations of the see-saw so that first one and then the other functions in the leadership position.

When you have a marked difference in how responsible the two partners are, you will quite likely find that even a moderate increase in stress will trigger the underfunctioning spouse into dysfunction. This means that the underfunctioning spouse can quite easily fall into any form of physical illness, emotional illness such as depression, phobia, or other mental disorders, or irresponsible antisocial behavior such as alcohol or substance abuse, violence, or other forms of acting out. In many ways, an unbalanced responsibility pattern in the family is the real source of the dysfunctional behavior. Just as we need to keep our bodies in balance to maintain our physical health, so we also need to keep our family responsibilities in balance in order to maintain emotional equilibrium.

Family therapists know that one effective way to help a family in which there is a dysfunctional spouse is to encourage the over-functioning partner to assume *less* of the responsibility. In families where alcoholism is present, for example, the nondrinking spouse has often assumed too much of the burden for maintaining the family. If this overresponsible partner can learn to take on less of that respon-sibility, the see-saw will right itself and the previously dysfunctional spouse will often become more responsible. Amazing, but it does work, as many families of recovering alcoholics discover.

Dependence and Co-Dependence

Dependence is a universal human characteristic. We are social animals and our lives intertwine in various complex ways. Some aspects of our dependencies are realistic and natural. We are all limited in many ways. There are just some things we cannot manage to do alone, so we might as well be humble and admit those limitations. Realistic dependence differs from unhealthy overdependence, however. At times, we may overestimate our supposed "need" for one another and end up feeling more dependent than is realistic. Sometimes, when we feel we can-not do something alone, we tend to feel sorry for ourselves and lonely.

Sometimes that is just a feeling and not a realistic fact. Many times, even though we are afraid that we cannot do something, in fact we can find ways to manage to get the job done.

I talked with a blind man I met on the bus in Boston, with his curly haired brown dog nestled under our feet. He told me the two most important things for him about coping: "Have a good dog and use your initiative." Despite his realistic dependence on his seeing eye dog, this man had a sense of mastery and independence. Often we can use our initiative and find people we can hire or barter with, although I do not mean to imply that finding help is always easy; far from it. Finding the right people to help us with tasks we cannot manage alone is one of the most challenging aspects of coping.

Often our feelings of dependence go down deep into the unconscious and our personal life history. In our childhood, we were all incapable and realistically dependent for a very long time. While we were growing up, we really needed people to care for us. Sometimes we didn't get enough of what we needed. Sometimes we were hurt and there was no one to take the pain away. We felt lost and desolate. If there were larger gaps in the amount of care we received, for example, long times in infancy or early childhood when we felt abandoned and alone, then as adults we tend to have a prolonged feeling that we need others to care for us. This is unrealistic dependence.

When you are caught in a state of unrealistic dependence, you may feel that your whole world will fall apart if there isn't someone there to give you emotional support. You may feel incompetent, inadequate, or even quite lost. This is a very deep and painful feeling, one that many people would prefer not to have; but if you try to run from your dependency feelings, you tend to stay caught there, without being able to resolve your situation. So, can you admit that there are times when you are a "klutz," times when you say all the wrong things, times when you fall down on the job? If you can honestly admit those things to yourself *without losing your self-esteem*, that is, without giving up a basic sense of your own value and worth, then you are far along the road to managing your dependency conflicts. When you can admit your limitations but still know your value and strengths, then you are quite likely to be able to cope effectively without being unnecessarily dependent on others.

When relationships are going poorly, one common cause is an emotional state between the two people that we call "co-dependence."

Co-dependent relationships can happen between spouses, or in other partnerships, or they can occur between parent and child. In co-dependent relationships both partners are in some ways dysfunctional. Rather than living in a partnership based on shared strengths, they tend to operate out of an emotional state that emphasizes their pooled weaknesses. Often one partner in this duo plays the "needy" role while the other partner, who outwardly seems strong, is actually coming from an emotional state of "needing to be needed." Neither is free or able to operate well alone. Their pattern is similar to the underfunctioning and overfunctioning pair described earlier; their see-saw is out of balance.

An example may help to clarify this pattern of overdependence. A student came for counseling early in her freshman year, not at all sure she would be able to make it in college. Jeanine, as I'll call her, looked like a little girl trying to play grown up. She was frail and fragile. Many times during our sessions she was unable to speak because she felt so overwhelmed and incompetent. She would sit tearfully before me and somehow I was supposed to guess what was bothering her. Gradually her story came out. Jeanine was frightened by her father and extremely dependent on her mother. She had come five hundred miles away, but she called home several times a day. While at college, she tended to idealize her mother, but whenever she spent time at home, she came back very anxious. Her mother would be "kind" and "sympathetic" and she would "take care of" Jeanine, but this was at the cost of emphasizing her daughter's incompetence. Mother "knew" that Jeanine needed her; she could not afford to let Jeanine cope with college on her own. Jeanine's dependence and her mother's need to be needed kept them caught in a dysfunctional pattern.

Jeanine started to fall behind in her school work. There was no one at college who would tell her when to study. Her professors began to worry about her. It soon became quite clear that she was so inherently dependent and waif-like that she was able to manipulate even her college professors into taking care of her. But there are limits to such dependence in the real world of adult living. Soon we discovered that Jeanine was flunking out. "Should I leave?" she asked me. She wanted me to make the choice for her. I tried to help her make that choice on her own. She asked her boyfriend, her mother, her roommate. Finally, Jeanine was able to make that one decision: she decided to leave school. She was too dependent, too needy to be able to cope with college away from home.

Adolescence is a time for breaking the dependent ties with home. Jeanine was not ready. Her mother had infantilized her too much, leaving her with a feeling of total incompetence. Mother's need to be needed left her daughter feeling unrealistically dependent. The same pattern sometimes happens in the homes of handicapped children. There too, beyond realistic dependence, they may develop family patterns of overdependence. Unrealistic dependence and presumed incompetence can lead to subtle manipulative demands: "Take care of me." To help a young person become adult, we may sometimes have to frustrate his or her desires to remain a child.

With relationships that are going well, there is less likely to be a power struggle over dependency needs. Such relationships are more likely to have a balance with each partner contributing a certain amount of nurturance. They also provide room for one another so that each one feels: "We are free to be, you and me." Particularly in marriage, there must be some degree of detachment and recognition of each one's individual differences. In all other close relationships, each partner must have room to be an individual. Each person is different with his or her own pattern of strengths and weaknesses. In any relationship, while it is reasonable to divide the labors and capitalize on individual strengths, the partners should never become so dependent that either of them loses his or her sense of competency. To evaluate the degree of dependency in your relationship, you might wonder: How competent do I feel? How fearful am I if I had to go it alone? How adjustable are we in our work and in our emotional interactions with each other? How can we best keep a balance?

When Illness Shifts the Balance

Many marital partners are quite comfortable with the degree of dependence they have on one another. Often they have adapted to one another, evolving a balance between their particular personality strengths and limitations. If one partner is especially strong as a thinker, for example, he or she may rely on a spouse who is more comfortable in the feeling world to deal with the emotional issues and provide empathy for the children. Conversely, the more emotionally sensitive spouse may be happy to leave the income tax records in the hands of the thinker.

A practical spouse may be highly competent in handling daily real-

ities in a here-and-now way, but may be less likely to look ahead and
see future possibilities or potential problems. In contrast, an intuitive
spouse may see quite clearly what is likely to be coming ahead but may
be less adept in managing daily practical matters. The intuitive one
may be very effective as a planner, but he or she may prefer to leave
the arrangements for car repairs to the more here-and-now, practical
spouse. Such arrangements work quite well when the strengths of the
pair balance one another.

When illness strikes a family, however, it disrupts their accustomed
balance. When one member of the couple succumbs to major disability
or death, the balance that has been present in the family necessarily
shifts. The partner must cope with this shift, and the need to find a
new type of balance is one of the most crucial aspects of illness for the
family.

When a family faces a medical emergency, there are tangible physical effects they must cope with but, in addition, there are usually
psychological reactions that may add to the family stress and difficulties in coping. A stroke or automobile accident, for example, may result
in brain damage that affects the patient's thinking capacity. This disruption is sometimes dramatic but, more often, it is subtle and difficult
to perceive. Any disruption at all in thinking capacity of a dominant,
previously overfunctioning spouse will affect the dependency balance
in the whole family. For example, a high-income accountant developed a neurological disorder that felt "like his brains were scrambled
eggs." His wife had to take over many of the thinking and wage-earning
functions in the family. Her time was less available for the family. In addition, there were, as always, emotional reactions to the accident that
affected the emotional balance in the family.

We know that depression and anxiety are common reactions a patient may have. These feelings will affect others, altering the emotional
tone in the couple and often in the whole family. Suppose you are in
a marriage where your spouse has always been a dominant or overfunctioning partner but suddenly he or she is taken seriously ill. How
will you cope? The shock of the illness may be very disruptive for a
while. Suddenly you must assume responsibility for which you feel in-
adequately prepared. While you try to offer as much support as possible
to the patient, you may feel acutely aware of the lack of social support
for yourself. You will need to learn new tasks and set new priorities.
Don't be surprised if you have occasional feelings of inadequacy and

dependence. Or you may feel angry that you are unavoidably in this caretaking position. Such feelings are normal and almost inevitable.

I recall the patients with Alzheimer's disease and the tremendous burden their families had to bear. Some of these men in the Day Hospital were as young as fifty, former professionals whose minds were now totally gone. Some could not remember their own children's names, how to dress themselves, how to eat or talk. One shuffled and drooled; but he was a nice man and still cared about the other patients. In his blue eyes and gentle expression, you could tell he cared. He had been a psychiatrist up until two years before. Illness spares no occupation. Even the great and mighty succumb. Another man was a building contractor, used to giving orders and having his own way. He was strong, firm, and muscular. His brown hair kept falling over his eyes. He now wandered away from the hospital on a regular basis. He thrashed about in rages whenever he was confined. His family were beside themselves. How do you cope with a full-grown, raging man when his memory is gone and he has no comprehension, no logic or reasoning ability left? His rages and wanderings often happened in the middle of the night. His wife was so exhausted she sent him to the Day Hospital so that she could get some respite.

Whatever the persisting illness, you as the caretaking spouse will have to begin the long-term process of adaptation. To cope in such circumstances, you may need to learn or relearn many skills that your spouse previously handled. You will undoubtedly feel overwhelmed at times. You will need patience, willingness to grow and develop new skills, and a support network to help you master the necessary changes. This kind of dramatic change will be stressful, but you will have the opportunity to grow in personal competence as you gradually master the new challenges you have to face. It will be important to remember that you are *not* totally alone, even though you may feel that way at times. You will find a new balance and new ways to relate to others. While you may not be able to depend on your spouse as you have in the past, you do not have to pretend to be totally independent either.

We all know that independence, self-sufficiency, and self-direction are ingrained in the American value system. We must not forget, however, that joining together in groups to maximize our common welfare is also typically American. We are social by nature, so when we have illness or a physical disability ourselves or in a member of the family, we must accept this inevitable, realistic dependence. It is no cause for shame or stigmatizing. It is not true that rugged individualism is the essence of being human. As rehabilitation psychologists and disabled patients tell us, other values like dependability, interdependence, autonomy, freedom, control, and finding many, varied options are all positive aspects of living that we can value and actualize in many circumstances. It is of greater benefit to people with disabilities and their families if we think beyond the rigid picture of the individualist to a more flexible view of those who cope creatively, using all the resources available in the environment.

Communities for Adult Growth

As adults we all require nurturance from a wider environment as we step along the path of growth and individuation. We all need networks of friends for support in coping with the more difficult challenges of living. Communities or friendship networks also provide us with the everyday opportunities to be related, to learn, to bond emotionally with others, and to have a sense of belonging, which is so important in life. These are basic human needs that often cannot be met by families alone.

When a fire or flood destroys one's home, to whom does one turn for a place to stay? In the long months of clean-up and rebuilding, who will provide the emotional support as you work your way out of chaos and back to some semblance of normalcy? Many people in such emergency situations do not have extended family nearby. They may turn to a friendship network that centers around their church, synagogue, or other spiritual community. Fortunately, there is increasing pastoral awareness of the need for a deep sense of community and commitment to help families who have sudden emergency needs. Community means mutual caring for the whole body of people — for all their physical, emotional, and spiritual needs.

No one has yet fully expressed a modern definition of "community," but Scott Peck comes closest when he tells us that inclusion is a vital aspect of community welfare. A community that is open and welcoming provides a haven for all its members. Through community belonging and support, each person is able to cope with the stresses of life a bit more easily. In community, tolerance for human differences grows as people widen their hearts to one another. Each feels accepted and, in that environment of acceptance, each can grow into the unique and different person that he or she is meant to be. Exclusivity is the great enemy of community; it is critical, rejecting, and destructive. Exclusivity is elitist and therefore detrimental to forming the bonds that unite and maintain a caring community. It is not easy to grow in a community unless there is an atmosphere of openness, trust, and inclusivity.

St. Francis was a large suburban parish that was dedicated to forming a sense of community among its members. A creative, well-educated congregation worked well with their liberal pastor, a kindly, gentle, forthright man of about sixty, who had a touch of administrative genius and daring. One dynamic aspect of the development of community at St. Francis came about when the pastor hired young Fr. Joe to develop the religious education program and renew the worship services. Under his creative leadership, a core group of lay people developed into a powerful force, full of youthful enthusiasm. He trained many young parents first as Sunday School teachers and then as lay leaders to create vibrant, experimental worship services. The mood was one of enthusiastic self-discovery and renewal. The young adults who became parish leaders were excited by the new thinking to which they were exposed. They delved into scripture, theology, and psychology, finding personal meaning that they shared with one another whenever the community met to dialog. They talked together about the real issues of their lives, about the stresses they faced and the ways they were learning to cope.

Within St. Francis, variety and experimentation were encouraged and the energized parishioners worked, studied, played, and prayed together. Creativity blossomed as parents discovered how to reach youngsters through music, drama, storytelling, art, and dance. In this context, the psychological needs of both the adults and the children became a central concern of all who were involved. In this budding community, spirituality wore earthy attire. Learning about group dynamics as well as feelings and individual personality became daily discoveries as people discussed with one another what was happening in themselves, in their families, and in the wider community. The training of the parishioners had begun, based on experiential methods and much reflective thought. This mode of energetic involvement of the people was the heart of community that was to become, over the next fifteen years, a model parish.

In such a creative community, everyone knows that you are *gaining* far more from the process of involvement than you give in terms of hours and effort. When the community emphasizes personal growth through group process, you have the opportunity to learn about yourself and others. You make the commitment to get involved and your challenge becomes how to welcome and involve others. You may struggle with other community members on understanding the issues. You may share your concerns about how to apply your faith to the practical decisions each of you have to make in this late twentieth-century world. The ethics of business and the problems of raising children become the real issues that people discuss. How to find time for your own psychological needs and spiritual nourishment are other topics that are likely to enter the dialog. How to help your neighbor can lead to lively discussions about the issues of poverty, racism, sexism, and other forms of discrimination. Social action for the betterment of the larger world is likely to become a commitment.

Ministry and ecumenical outreach flourish at St. Francis. They send representatives to interfaith activities and are regular volunteers at soup kitchens and other services for the poor. In altruistic ways, this group helps many others to cope. Peace and justice issues throughout the world always stir community support. Many have been involved in visiting the hospital or other homebound people to offer counsel and support. When Bob, one of their own members, became disabled and housebound, the community set up a weekly schedule for visits, which they have faithfully kept for many years. Bob is now in a wheelchair, and he seldom gets out of the house except when community members bring him to special services. Imagine the therapeutic effects of four or five friends visiting every week — not just at the beginning of an illness, or at holiday time, but consistently, faithfully being there over the years!

This commitment to one another and faithfulness in hardship is never more clearly evident than when there is a death in one of their families. Since several of the members have suffered from cancer fatalities, the community has integrated the hospice approach into their way of being with one another. At such times, the dying member and his or her family have been the center of extended community support. In one family, while Evelyn, the wife, went out to work to provide income for their five children, other volunteer community members took over the caretaking of her husband, Ben. As he lay dying, they sat with him and shared memories of the years they had worked and played and worshiped together. The love and time they spent with their dying member provided comfort and enrichment, not only for the distressed family, but for all the participating community members as well. The community became extended family for Evelyn, Ben, and their children. Each member grieved and felt the poignant reality of the loss they all deeply experienced. In such generosity they came to realize the full meaning of the fact that giving is a blessing to the giver as well as to the grateful receivers. This kind of community support provides emotion-focused coping opportunity to the fullest degree.

The community at St. Francis changed over the years, serving as a training ground, not just for the laity but for their pastoral leaders as well. Just as the congregation was learning what it means to be involved with one another, so too the various clergy who served them were also learning. They became notably more relaxed with the parishioners, able to laugh, to be open and comfortable with the people. They learned what it means to empower the parishioners, to have an active, vital congregation. Although power struggles happened occasionally, the people and clergy worked these conflicts through because of their commitment and loving dedication to the community. All the members learned and grew and supported one another. The leaders also found a deeper understanding of the needs, the gifts, the interests, and the variability of the members. Together they shared all aspects of community living; they learned how to actualize new creative possibilities; and they learned about intimacy in their struggle to form community. They worked together and got to know one another in men's groups, women's groups, prayer and study groups, retreats and pot-luck suppers. They learned to love one another and to tolerate their differences. This deep experiential learning was undoubtedly the most productive outcome of the renewal at St. Francis.

As Scott Peck tells us, a community is a group that has come to transcend its individual differences. Learning how to work together in community takes time, and that gift of one's time requires commitment. When we talk about transcending differences, that does not mean obliterating or demolishing the differences among people. Rather it means to surpass or to extend beyond the limits of those differences. Those very human differences that so often keep us separated from one another are to be cherished and valued. The key to transcendence within a group is the *appreciation of differences*. A group becomes a community, in part, because its members do not try to ignore, deny, hide, or change their differences. Rather than try to change one another (an attempt inevitably doomed to failure), the members of a community celebrate their differences and consider them gifts to be valued.

A community that values variability within itself also tends to value other groups that differ in many ways. Outreach and an appreciation of many different viewpoints tend to mark the humanistic characteristics of a vibrant community. The variability and pluralism of a community is one essential aspect of its vitality. Peck writes, "If 'one world' meant a melting pot in which everything comes out a bland mush instead of a salad of varied ingredients and textures — I'm not sure that outcome would be palatable. The solution lies in the opposite direction: in learning how to appreciate — yea, celebrate — individual, cultural and religious differences and how to live with reconciliation in a pluralistic world."

So far, we have been reflecting on a community that is generally open-minded, exploring new ideas and developing responses to the social challenges going on around them. Not all communities or institutions are as open-minded, but even when they are, there are always interpersonal challenges and forces within the group that we can learn to understand and work around. Even in an open community, new ideas often meet with heated discussion, sometimes with anger, tears, or fears expressed within the group. When there is commitment to one another, along with commitment to one's own growth and change, the members tend to deepen their experience of life, and to broaden their outlook, developing compassion and empathy for others in the human family.

Working together in groups helps us grow in our understanding of emotional realities. We learn to understand our own emotions, what triggers our reactions and what triggers others to make the responses they do. While working together in groups may sometimes increase the level of stress we experience, we also have the potential to grow and learn from all of our experiences with one another in groups. Ultimately, this learning, along with the social support we receive, helps us to cope more effectively not only with our own emotions, but also with the feelings of others around us.

Human Systems: How They Work

A community, a family, or any group of three or more people comprises a human system. When we look deeper into human groups, we see all sorts of intertwining patterns of relating. Those patterns are well known: a few basic patterns are repeated again and again in all kinds of situations. In any group, along with what seems to be happening on the surface, there is also a great deal going on in repetitive patterns; patterns of which the participants are often not aware. Groups, like families, differ from one another in several systematic ways. The more we can understand the nature of human systems and how they operate, the more we can cope effectively both in our external work and social groups and at home in our families.

One way that groups differ from one another has to do with the amount of emotional closeness they display. At one extreme are systems that we call "fused." A fused system is very intensely interrelated, as though people are blended, enmeshed, or melted together. Feelings may seem to be very loving when stress levels are low, but when stresses increase, the fused system tends to become dysfunctional. There is an emotional contagion that happens in fused systems that can be acutely uncomfortable for all the members who are present. I imagine you have experienced this kind of scenario: one person walks into a group in an angry mood, and all of a sudden the whole group is angry and quarreling with one another. Or one person feels anxious and the anxiety spreads until the whole group wants to move to do something quickly, and/or to get away from one another. Emotional contagion is very characteristic of fused systems.

At the other extreme are systems that are "distant." Such systems have great difficulty relating to one another at all. A distant group, like a distant family, tends to spend much of its time in individual, solitary activities. A lack of communication is the primary dysfunctional aspect of a distant system. No one seems to know what the others are doing. Planning is difficult and the rare times when the group comes together may be conflictual. Everyone wants to get away again as soon as possible.

You may have noticed that the systems I have described as fused or distant parallel the old two-step pursuit-and-distance, which I discussed earlier. There are certainly many similarities between what happens in the relationship of two people and what happens in a larger social group. When groups are fused, there may be too much intense, uncomfortable emotionality. But when groups distance (just like the distancing individual), there is a lonely, unsupported, uncommunicative quality that can be equally uncomfortable and dysfunctional. Groups, like individuals, have the capacity to move closer or to become more distant. When you watch what is happening in your group, you may learn to intervene to keep the group more in balance. Everyone is more comfortable in a group that is neither too fused nor too distant.

The leadership of any group, whether family, community, or larger institution, is a key element in how the group will develop its own unique style. How open, how energetic, how creative is the group? How plodding, heavy, or frustrating is the group style? Much depends on the leaders, but the personalities of the group members also have significant impact.

Behavior patterns within groups tend to echo each member's patterns in the family that he or she grew up in. Interpersonal *triangles*, in particular, tend to play out patterns we all know from childhood. Imagine yourself with two childhood friends, let's call them Bill and Phoebe. (You can substitute any other names that make this triangle ring true for you.) With the three of you, who pairs up with whom? Do Bill and Phoebe become friends, leaving you feeling left out and alone? Do you play up to Bill and try to see that Phoebe gets left behind as soon as possible? Or do you and Phoebe go off, leaving Bill to sulk or do his own thing? Or are you the group peacemaker? What happens when Bill and Phoebe get into an argument: Do you perpetually try to get them to work it out? Are you forever caught in trying to make this system into a harmonious group?

When you think back into your childhood, this kind of scenario may have been repeated endlessly with friends, like Bill and Phoebe, or with your siblings. More often than not, triangles echo many interrelated patterns that occurred between yourself, your siblings, and one or both of your parents. When you come to know yourself quite well, you realize that many of the patterns with your work colleagues, friends, and family today mirror those same old patterns you played out in earlier days.

From time to time, we all get caught in triangular patterns. They are inevitable and cause a great deal of the stress and misery that we see in human systems. If you are in a three-person system, even if it is a subgroup of a larger system, you will recognize the triangle by the emotional intensity of your interaction with the two other people. There is one secret that family therapists have to teach us about how to cope with triangles. The key is to remember that you have just two responsibilities: you need to relate to Bill and you need to relate to Phoebe. *Your responsibility is to get along as well as possible with each of the other two people, individually. Anything else that happens is not your concern.* If Bill and Phoebe fight, that's not your concern. (A tremendous amount of stress occurs when a well-meaning person tries to get two people to get along with each other. You see it in families all the time: Mother says "Love your brother; don't fight!" How often do the children listen to her?) It is also not your responsibility to get involved in any two-against-one movements in the triangle. If Bill and Phoebe go off, leaving you alone, you will have to find some way to cope with your own loneliness, but that's not likely to happen if you do your job of relating well to Bill and to Phoebe, each on a one-to-one relationship basis.

In any system we are in, we tend to mirror the patterns of behavior we learned in our parental homes. Our parents set up the family the way they learned it from *their* parents. On back through the ages, there is a multigenerational process in families. Cultural beliefs, values, and behavior patterns are all recurrent themes that have had strong influence on who we are. For each of us, the family history is very influential. That system tends to get played out, again and again, in the groups where we are involved.

In larger organizations, group dynamics take on more complex forms, but it is helpful to use the metaphor of the family in order to understand what is going on. Big organizations are like large families, with leaders taking on parental roles and colleagues acting like siblings. You will find triangles, patterns of pursuit and distance, and habits of overfunctioning and underfunctioning wherever you turn. When you begin to study systems in process, the essence of learning lies in *awareness*. Watch, listen, and feel what is going on. Listen not only to the content of what people say but to the feelings that go along with it. Hear the undercurrent, the music under the lyrics. You can train yourself to become aware.

When you recognize conflicts within organizations and struggles for power, the root cause is usually based on the emotional needs of the contenders. Coping with such conflictual situations is often stressful. However, if you remember the dynamics of the triangle, that your responsibility is simply to relate to each side as well as you can, then your job will be easier to define. Since the nature of a system in conflict is to confuse, you will get frustrated sooner or later if you try to sort out all of the intrigue of organizational politics. It is far better and simpler to adopt a pose of mutual respect. Keep yourself calm and look for those people with whom you can be yourself in an open, mutually supportive way.

Coping the Relational Way

It is clear by now that relationships are for better or worse. The way of social support is an important way of coping, but its stream may run over rocky terrain. When friendships, family, and other relationships come to rocky places, many people are tempted to give it all up and say, "I'll go it alone." Retreat may be temporarily effective but it is not usually a good long-range solution. Riding the rapids of social relationships may be exciting or it may feel stressful. Everyone who relates to other people in the real world has periods of riding the rapids, but if you don't find yourself coming to calmer waters after a while, you need to ask yourself how well your network is working.

4

The Way of the Spirit

ARNOLD WAS A YOUNG BLACK COLLEGE STUDENT, very hand-some and talented. His parents and his teachers had given him so much. They had encouraged him, as he was beyond doubt a young man of great promise. He was brilliant on the saxo-phone and had chosen writing as his career goal. Since early childhood, Arnold had been helped by affirmative action programs, and he had been able to make the most of his potential. He was good at what he did: successful in college and clearly on his way toward a very productive life.

But now Arnold lay in a coma. The automobile accident was not his fault. While he was stopped for a traffic light, a reckless driver in a red Honda crashed into him from behind. Arnold never knew what hit him. Arnold lay in coma in the hospital for many months while the doctors and nurses worked on him. By now they knew his prognosis was poor. The doctors had to let the family know. Arnold was in PVS: a Persistent Vegetative State. "No, I'm sorry, Mrs. Jones, there will be no further improvement now. He will not come out of the coma. There's nothing else we can do. I'm sorry." The months of waiting with hope had come to an end. The medical staff had done all they could. Where could the family turn now in their grief?

As I listened to Mrs. Jones, I thought how much grief at such a time cries out loudly, desperate for relief. She needed human comfort, but human comfort is never enough. These are the times of wrenching pain when the whole of one's being cries out, "My God, how can this be?" This mother who had lost her son wondered about the meaning of her own life. Tearfully she asked, "What is the reason for life? What was the purpose of all those hours I spent on him? I loved him so much, gave him so much, and now it has all come to nothing." She wept, "My son is gone." And, perhaps even more poignantly, she asked, "What am I going to do now? What can I do with my love?" Much of her life

83

had been devoted to helping Arnold develop all his potentials, but she felt somehow she had failed him. Where would she invest her energies now? Where could she find new purpose and meaning in life? And what sense could she make of the life that her son lived, just as it was, cut all too short?

Words can never fully express the human tragedy that one encounters daily within the walls of medical centers. There, one meets courage and determination, side by side with fear and fragility. Dedicated love as well as frustration and anxieties are common experiences for patients, staff, and families alike. In a hospital community, everyone is striving; facing physical and emotional challenges to the limits of endurance. There are many successes, and that keeps hope alive; but the tragedies continue. In face of death or major disability, human effort seems ultimately inadequate.

Working in hospitals had a tremendous impact on me, and I became keenly aware of the strength of the human spirit. I saw how the major stresses of physical illness and disability strike, and how people reach down deep inside to find a hidden source of fortitude. Regardless of their upbringing or faith tradition, most people seek spiritual strength at such times of trauma. Even those who have stayed away many years from formal religious traditions tend to return to their spirituality to cope with the big crises. As people seek solace, sustenance, guidance, and healing, they begin to turn in their innermost hearts to prayer, meditation, or contemplation.

In this chapter we look at the Tao of coping from the perspective of spirit, that ephemeral connection that relates to the Divine by whatever name. As Carl Jung so often emphasized, the psychospiritual aspects of our quest for wholeness center on and are guided by a godlike aspect within us. This core Self is the ultimate concern of our human existence. From the Western theological tradition, this Self could be called the "immanent godhead." Chinese philosophy classically named this sacred interior space "Tao," viewed as a flow of life that moves irresistibly toward its goal. The goal and the way are both Tao, which can be understood as meaning fulfillment, wholeness, and a sense of reaching one's destination at each moment. When one's mission is done, the beginning and the end come together in a perfect realization of the meaning of existence. This Tao is believed to be innate in all things.

We can see there is great variety in the spiritual modalities that people call upon to help cope with suffering and with the elements of life that are beyond personal control. As we look at these spiritual practices, we'll gain a new perspective on the wide-ranging ways that people call upon their innate spiritual resources. In this country, well over 90 percent of the population admits to some belief in God, but many tend to be fiercely independent about their own private and communal forms of worship. Buddhists and Christians, for example, still have great difficulty in their attempts to dialog together about spiritual matters. Moslems and Jews still tend to fiercely defend their differences even though they may also admit their commonalities. Some spiritual paths are theistic, and some are not. I discuss most extensively the Western Judeo-Christian tradition because that is what I know the best. In the very rich diversity of our unique spiritual quests, there are also common threads. My aim is simply to present a glimpse at the variety of spiritual resources, so that we can sense the richness and the unifying threads of spirituality.

In discussing spirituality, when I use the word "we," I am speaking from the perspective of "the believer" but also from the viewpoint of "the seeker," one who has begun the spiritual search. Especially when weathering the crises, people with a spiritual orientation often rely on inner experience of transcendent reality, and this helps them to cope even with extraordinary difficulties. People in trouble tend to seek a Deity (however defined) who can touch them personally, a Deity who can help them transcend the human tragedy and renew the essence of life.

Prayer

Naomi talked about what prayer meant to her in scriptural terms. She said, "You know God told Noah to build the ark and *then* He sent the flood. God wouldn't send the flood until the ark was ready. I often think about that when I pray. I trust that whatever 'floods' may threaten to overwhelm me, it won't be more than I can handle. I am being held in that ark. When I pray, I trust in God's promises, and I visualize myself being held safe and secure. Even though I may be tossed about by stormy seas, like Noah was, I will come through the experience stronger than before. I trust in God's covenant and the rainbow that sealed that promise."

Naomi knew that in the experience we call prayer a person can bring forth the big questions and seek to comprehend and master the terror and confusion of suffering. In prayer, one can ask some of the most basic of questions: How can there be such pain, misery, and injustice on the earth? How can there be a God of goodness when the suffering is so great?

It has been said that everyone prays. Even the denial of God, or anger at God, is a statement of relationship or some belief. It is said, if ever you whisper a wish for understanding or help, or a desire for something or someone beyond to sustain you, whether or not you call it "prayer," you are praying. In or out of formal religion, people pray whenever they seek inwardly for strength. Whether or not they address a Being called "God," all people behave in ways that believers refer to as "prayer." The spiritual life is deep and personal.

No one can truly understand another's prayer experience, but we can try it on for size. Ann and Barry Ulanov describe prayer in terms of talking with the inner truest self. In prayer, one speaks with total honesty. We begin with who we are — not who we want to be or who someone thinks we should be, but who we really are. Speaking with this essential honesty, we then listen for the response of a deeper, truer Wisdom. In prayer we extend beyond our known resources, reaching out to the unknown God.

For example, Adrian prays from her deepest longing, reaching out for what she vaguely senses is beyond her. "O Mother of creation, help me find you. Help me to find and to grow in your love. I am like a seed in the garden, waiting for your sunshine to bring me to life; waiting for your rain to wash me and nourish me into growth. O Creator, enlarge my desire and my heart until I can grow big enough to receive your desire, your Holy Spirit. Permeate my being with your Being. Grow me into union with you."

There are many types of prayer, but the essential ingredient in all prayer experience is this desire for communion with an all-sufficient One. Prayerful people from many religious traditions have found the experience of the best and truest inner core of ourselves is mirrored in the vast wonder, the Ideal of all humanity. In the tradition of Zen Buddhism, this reflective experience is called the Divine Mirror. The soul mirrors the Divine; endlessly the reflection goes back and forth. At the highest levels of Christian mysticism, the experience is similar. People who have devoted their lives to the spiritual quest have come to recognize that it is the inner truest, godlike part of ourselves that prays, reflects, and listens to the Transcendent Being that is known as God.

Another way to describe the process of prayer is that it is spirit communing with Spirit. Our inner core being, what Carl Jung calls Self, prays in an essential effort to communicate with something greater, something beyond. In prayer, the most dynamic, creative, inspiring aspect of our deepest person is the spirit that reaches out to contact the more universal, transcendent Being that we call God.

When we look more concretely at the various types of prayer, we can see the ways our prayer life can develop. The most common form of prayer involves *petition* or *supplication*. Prayers of petition usually begin in childhood, often with simple, self-interested requests: "O God, let it be sunny on my birthday"; or "Make me hit a home run"; or "Help me to do well on the test I have next period"; or "Let the boy down the block like me"; or "Please don't let Mommy punish me." Prayer is a simple, natural way for children to cope when they come to realize the world is not always the way we want it to be. These simple prayers of childhood are the forerunners of the heartfelt, poignant requests of adulthood in which we express and test our faith. Especially in times of trial, despair, and desperation, we cope by turning with childlike faith to an omnipotent Deity when we fervently pray: "Help me to have the strength to get through this crisis!"; "Bless my children!"; "Please make him stop drinking!"; "Grant me guidance, show me how to cope"; "Fill my heart with love"; "Help me to forgive."

Many people who are not familiar with the subtle varieties of prayer think that supplication — asking God for something we want — is immature or foolish, but this is not necessarily so. Although it certainly is true that religion can be used as a crutch, prayers of petition *can* be mature, natural, and appropriate in many circumstances. For example, Jeannette prays by petitioning Jesus for help in relation to her work situation, which has become tumultuous because of a difficult, authoritarian boss: "O Jesus, gentle love, help me in this time of need. Help me to remain calm, yet strong. Help me to respond wisely to his incessant demands. And please, Jesus, help him too. Help him to understand me and the efforts I am making. Take away his anxiety and the hostility he is aiming at me and others. Help us to come to some deeper levels of acceptance and to find ways to work effectively together. Guide us toward peace."

There is a great difference between giving up helplessly, which is

immature, and the realistic recognition of our limitations and need for
God. After doing the best they can, many people with a spiritual orientation still feel a need for something beyond themselves. Then it is
time to look honestly into the depths of self and call for the resources
beyond merely human capacities. Trying to ignore our limitations with
a stiff upper lip does not help. To cope, to become truly mature, we
must certainly develop all the human capacities we have available. But
then, recognizing our limitations and weaknesses, we can also turn to
God for further wisdom, understanding, and power. Put another way, it
helps to think: *Work like it's all up to me, and pray like it's all up to God.*

As believing adults we pray for others, and we pray for our own
deepest needs. We pray for situations that are out of our own control,
and we pray for the grace to do our best. We pray for strength, emotional relief, and wisdom, and for a deepening relationship with the
Being we know as God.

In Manhattan there's a spiritual center just one flight up off a very
busy corner on Broadway. The center is a very serene place, but right
outside are all the flashing lights and traffic noises of New York City.
It's quite a contrast: inner peace and outer turmoil. One day Kathy
told us there, "Several people I know pray whenever they hear a siren
go by. A siren always indicates someone is in trouble, and prayers we
offer may help to relieve their suffering." That brought new meaning
to the city sounds we were hearing.

We essentially are using prayers of petition whenever we think
deeply about another person and wish that person well. We often whisper petitions silently, even wordlessly, in the privacy of our own hearts.
We can also share these supplications, however. *Shared group prayer*
seems to have added spiritual power whenever people join together,
with hearts united, raising similar hopes, wishes, and pleas. Shared
prayer fosters a sense of unity and solidifies faith that may otherwise
waver. Common belief in the efficacy of prayer offers support to each
person who prays.

In addition to private and small group prayer, the next most common form of prayer is *liturgical* or *communal worship.* Such worship
or ritual expresses the prayer life of a community. When like-minded
believers come together, their prayer can be rich and full. From primor-
dial times, rites and rituals were originally designed to communicate
the beliefs and heartfelt prayers of the group members. To the beat of
shamanic drums, primal peoples in all regions have sought the inter-

vention of divine spirits to protect their tribe. It is a rich and powerful experience to recall or reenact these ancient forms of worship.

Unfortunately, today's worship services all too often fall far short of expressing the prayers of the people. If communal prayer is to work well, the presiding leader (whether minister, rabbi, priest, or other spiritual leader) needs to be fully aware of the thoughts, needs, and emotions of the worshiping community. Without a constant interchange between clergy and congregation, worship services become lifeless, rote, and boring. But a leader who is in touch with the feelings of the people can bring vibrancy to the worship experience.

In some cases, a congregation sacrifices authenticity and originality for the sake of familiarity. They may say rote prayers, repeating memorized words or sounds without any thought or meaning. While repetition of rote phrases has a place in the spiritual life of meditation, too often rote prayer leaves people feeling uninvolved. In contrast to this lack of involvement with habitual prayers, *spontaneous prayer* is frequently lively. Once people learn how to overcome their inhibition, they usually participate warmly. Whether in private prayer, small group, or congregational prayer gatherings, when prayer is spontaneous, it generates emotional involvement and thoughtful reflection. People speak from the heart and they speak openly as they pray aloud. "God, bless our community. Bless our loved ones. Heal us. Help us. Grant us peace in our world, peace in our families, peace and serenity in our hearts."

Sometimes prayer bubbles up from the unconscious and you may find yourself singing spiritual songs. "God, send forth your Spirit, and renew the face of the earth" is a phrase from a song that, like many others, sometimes bubbles up for me in an expression of prayer in the form of *music*. Like King David of the Old Testament, who composed psalms to the tune of harp and lyre, we pray when we sing or when we recite Psalms. Imagine the ancient Hebrew worshipers who sang together with deep resonance in their voices: "Your word is a lamp to guide me, and a light for my path. . . . Accept my prayers of thanks, Lord, and teach me your commands."

It has been said that "one who sings prays twice." In both Eastern and Western religious traditions, songs or chants often produce resonance that echoes deep within the psyche. Music cuts through the wordiness of our thoughts and adds impact to the meaning of the words. The song "Amazing Grace," for example, has great potency because of the power of the music, far beyond the mere words. Music can also arise, almost angelically, from the deep unconscious to bring its message of faith, hope, and consolation. You might want to notice, to listen well to the songs that spring forth spontaneously as you go about your daily tasks; this inner music is the language and the medium of spirit.

In prayer at the deeper levels, our conscious and unconscious minds are in communion. We quiet ourselves, and we wait. There is an unfolding. We feel in tune. At such deep moments, our prayers have special power. Prayer for *healing* often arises from such moments. This is a particular form of petition, one in which we are seeking wholeness for ourselves or others. Full health means a balance of all the physical systems and psychological forces that come together within the individual. When you think about what it means to be healthy, you realize the whole body's systems must be sensitively attuned: psychological, physiological, chemical, and electrical processes must be synchronized. A person who asks for healing is seeking to rebalance the psychosomatic systems as a whole.

Healing means different things, depending on the person and on the balance appropriate to his or her stage of life. For example, healing may involve acceptance. Peter, a paraplegic, may be "healed" when he comes to accept a wheelchair and to feel comfortable with the new lifestyle that requires of him. Ester, a stroke patient, may be "healed" when she realizes that she has much living left to do, even though she is partially paralyzed and unable to speak. She may still delight in knowing her grandchildren. She is still able to communicate in many nonverbal ways. While one person may be "fully healed" of an illness, for another the healing may take the form of eliminating a depression or anxiety associated with the illness.

Ginny, who had suffered extensively with her husband's lengthy illness, came to realize that even death may be a "healing," that is, a release from the burden of pain when a patient's life has come to a natural completion. Ginny's prayers for healing helped her husband to let go and die more peacefully; healing also came for herself in that her profound fears of loneliness were put to rest; and their relationship with one another was healed by an opening to deeper, more personal communications during their last days together.

A relationship may be healed whenever we learn new ways of understanding, compassion, or reconciliation, or when we open to one another, showing our vulnerabilities and coming to new levels of acceptance and intimacy. All these are the results we may hope for — and we are never sure exactly which will come — when we pray for healing.

Many people wonder how effective their prayers can possibly be. Ann and Barry Ulanov reflect on answers to prayer, describing the many ways in which prayer has influence, not only on others and external situations, but also on the person who prays. For example, there is an enlivening feeling that results from time spent in prayer. Our thoughts seem to expand; life itself expands. So prayer can uplift us, making us reverent, but it can also keep us humble. Then we may discover one of the real benefits of prayer is that *we are kept from burning out*. So often, our good intentions get us overcommitted and exhausted. When that happens, our capacity for compassion and empathy for others runs thin. Without prayer, our good will may eventually dwindle and disappear. Through prayer we become less pretentious, less inflated by our illusion that we can do it all. Prayer keeps us humble but committed, by connecting us to a larger power, strengthening our faith.

By humility I do not mean breast-beating, abject, self-flagellation. Rather, genuine humility is a truthful self-assessment that includes both our strengths and weaknesses. We begin to have compassion for our own limitations. In comparison to our own human weaknesses, we marvel at the transcendent power of the divine life that lives within us and around us. This experience of contrast is what we feel as *awe*. An overwhelming feeling of reverence may overtake us. The natural response is to lift the heart and mind in gratitude and praise.

Some claim that prayers of *praise* are the most powerful form of prayer life. The psalms of the Old Testament, for example, are full of sung praises for God. When we raise our thoughts to praise of the Divine, our hearts are lifted as well. Joy begins to bubble up. This is a psychological reality. The power of the evangelical churches, for example, is psychologically based on the experience of profound uplift that worshipers feel in the presence of a praising community, even when it arrives through the television medium. This real linkage of the experience of praise for the Deity and uplift of the human spirit has been verified by the experience of multitudes of praying people. Prayers of praise appear to touch the deep levels of our collective experience. From this place, this collective unconscious place, to use Jung's phrase, our experience is ultimately one of unification with people of faith throughout the ages.

Prayers of praise may coincide with or lead into the experience of contemplation, which we will discuss later. Spiritual writers generally say that praise is a higher form of prayer that usually develops at a more mature level than simple supplication. The ancient Hebrew prayer "Alleluia" is one of the simplest forms of praise. Many times we naturally combine praise with prayers of gratitude and expressions of love. In praise, many people believe the Holy Spirit moves within, filling one's own spirit with prayer and with the desire for union with the Divine. One such aspirant, Michael, privately prays: "O God, you are all goodness. Unite me to yourself. Use me to fulfill your purposes. Fill me with the abundance of your grace. You are ALL my heart desires. You are the Ground of all Being. Alleluia. Praised be God forever."

It seems that the experience of awe combines with love in the higher forms of prayer. At this point, one is far beyond simply praying in order to cope with life. The person who prays in this manner experiences an uplift; a significant inner change has taken place as a result of the prayers of praise. Many people report feeling a similar combination of awe and love at the more advanced stages of meditation as well.

Meditation

Janice sat in my office with her feet curled under her on the couch. She talked about another student, slightly older than herself, whom she admired immensely. What was it about this other young woman that made her so special? She said Kim was a poet, and very intelligent and articulate. But there seemed to be something more. Janice herself was a musician, so the creative dimension was something both these young women possessed in equal abundance. Was it a sexual desire? Janice was lesbian and Kim was not. No, Janice was quite sure that her admiration for Kim did not have sexuality at its root. No, there was something else special about Kim: she would sometimes talk about Japan and the feeling was not the same as other students who expressed admiration for the Japanese business acumen. This was something deeper, simpler. In one of her poems, Kim had written about the beauty of a single flower in a Japanese flower arrangement. As we explored that feeling, finally the essence began to emerge: Kim was a *meditator*, a practitioner of Zen. Her sense of simplicity, serenity, centeredness — that was what Janice so admired. "That's it," said Janice, snapping her fingers and pointing excitedly. That was what Janice was seeking for her own life. She would begin. Somewhere, somehow, she would learn to meditate so that she, too, could find the serenity that so graced her friend Kim.

There are many forms of meditation, and Herbert Benson, a Harvard physician, has catalogued some of the methods that he finds are most useful for medical patients. His book *The Relaxation Response* describes numerous ways to adapt Eastern meditation techniques in a nonreligious format in order to reduce stress and alter the Type A personality drive that is so common in cardiac patients, among others. Many of these methods are based on what is known as *single-pointed concentration.* Meditation teachers generally suggest that you set aside twenty minutes twice a day. They suggest that in meditating, you sit in a comfortable, erect pose and focus attention on a single object (visual mode), sound (auditory mode), or bodily sensation (kinesthetic mode).

The aim of meditation is to quiet the mind. Our minds are otherwise very busy with multiple thoughts and images that go on incessantly in normal waking consciousness. This mental busyness is what the Zen monks refer to as the "ten thousand things" that constantly preoccupy the mind. When you practice meditative techniques for a period of time, you enter an altered state of consciousness. Brain researchers recognize this shift in consciousness by the appearance of alpha brain waves supplanting the beta waves of ordinary awake states.

Patricia Carrington, a Princeton psychologist, has written a wonderfully compact description of the mental processes that occur during meditation. Her book *Freedom in Meditation* describes the varieties of techniques and the ways in which a *meditative mood* may emerge. The meditative state is striking in its tendency to go its own way, she says, sometimes not at all in the direction the meditator might anticipate. We may learn all the correct procedures of a particular form of meditation and still be surprised at the outcome. An altered state of consciousness *may* emerge — or other things may happen. These surprising "other things" include temporary physical or psychological effects. We may notice various physical tremors, twitches, or other sensations that may be either pleasant or uncomfortable. Psychological side effects can be mental states other than the peaceful state that we would expect: such unexpected states as a new awareness of our own frustrations, tensions, anxieties, or inadequacies.

If we do not understand what is happening, these effects can be dis-
couraging to the beginning meditator. I remember as a teenager when
I made my first attempts at meditation, my flitting mind convinced me
that I was failing and I gave up the process. Only much later did I
realize these effects are normal and are not reason to discontinue meditative practice. Psychologist and healer Joyce Goodrich calls these side
effects "white bears" (as in: "If you're told not to think about a white
bear, what do you suppose you'll think about?"). The solution is simply
to notice these side effects, realize they are temporary, and bring the
mind back to its object of focus. With time and practice, the meditative mood will arise more easily and it will gradually become deeper,
more sustained and rewarding.

In learning how to meditate, some people find it useful to try various techniques before settling down to the one method that is most
satisfying. What all techniques have in common is the aim of closing
out the distractions of the outer world. In meditation, we remove attention from the distracting sense impressions and thoughts to create
a kind of inner empty space. When the distractions of the outer world
are put in the distant background, we begin to feel that meditation is
taking effect. We feel calm and centered. We begin to have a sense of
inner balance.

Then we may become aware of a special kind of free-floating attention and begin to recognize the meditative mood. Words and logical
thoughts seem far less important. When deeply in the meditative
mood, we feel completely absorbed by the object of concentration.
Each time something else comes to mind, we simply become aware of
it as it drifts in and then drifts away again. There is a sort of faraway,
vague quality to the experience.

One very effective method of meditation is based on the use of a
mantra technique. This is the popular approach Transcendental Meditation (TM) teaches, and its style is very similar to the repetition of
rote prayers that various religious groups traditionally have handed
down over the ages. In mantra meditation, we select a word or phrase
(or you may be given one if you are working with a spiritual director or
teacher). It should be brief, not emotionally loaded, and sonorous when
repeated aloud. Some examples are "Om"; "Alleluia"; "All"; "Aum mani
padme hum"; "Jesus"; and "Lord Jesus Christ, have mercy." Longer
forms of rote prayers such as the "Hail Mary" and the "Lord's Prayer"
and the "Shema" may also serve as similar meditative methods. Once

the word or phrase is selected, we repeat it reverently over and over, attempting to concentrate on the sound. Naturally, our minds will wander. When that happens and we become aware that once again we have strayed, we should bring the mind gently back. Like a kindly parent, our aim is to watch the mind, gently curbing its tendency to wander. Again and again, bring the mind back, refocusing on the sound and the inner resonance. Nothing else matters. For a designated period of time, we sit until we almost become the sound. Rest into the sound. Deeply rest and allow the sounds to reverberate within.

Other auditory meditation techniques include concentration on the sound of chimes or on a lovely piece of music. Outdoors we can meditate on trills and calls of birdsong. By the water, I like to meditate on the sound of waves lapping or crashing against a shore. And at home, I have a lovely Tibetan gong that I ring three times whenever I enter or leave my home. This brief practice reminds me to return to a state of contemplation or here-and-now awareness.

As we examine the various meditative techniques, we can see that meditation has long been a common part of the experience of many people even when they do not recognize or name it as such. Fishermen, for example, may be in a meditative mood when they allow their minds to relax and simply absorb the sound of the waves. Visual forms of meditation may also be common in people who do not realize that they are meditating. Staring at a fire, or watching ripples on a pond, or contemplating fish swimming in a softly lighted tank are deeply relaxing experiences that often lead to the meditative mood. We now have scientific evidence for the therapeutic effects of such simple daily sitting in terms of relief from stress and benefits for coping.

So we recognize now that there are numerous opportunities for spontaneous meditative experiences, but it is also still helpful to include some formal meditation time in our daily plans. If we wait for the meditative mood simply to happen, we may remain so caught in the stresses of daily living that we never find the inner peace for which we yearn. When a young mother gazes in the face of her firstborn child nursing at the breast, she may experience the deeply satisfying meditative mood. But later in life when she has two or three young ones clamoring for her attention, she may find it much harder to get needed "alone-time." Three to five minutes, once or twice a day, may be all she can manage. But how much she needs that time!

In order to provide space in our busy lives, we must realize that meditation is wonderfully beneficial for coping with challenges, and we need to give ourselves permission to make it a priority. Meditation is a state of mind that each of us can cultivate if we will. To do so there are great varieties of methods from which to choose.

Among the most accessible methods are the *visual* meditations. Visual forms of meditation center on allowing our eyes to remain focused on a single object. A flower, for example, or a picture, or some artwork with symbolic meaning can be the focus of attention. In Christianity, meditation on the image of the cross, in Hinduism imaging the open lotus blossom, or in Buddhism, concentration on the rich images of a mandala are traditional forms of religious meditation. These often carry with them symbolic meaning, but that is not necessary. One can attain a meditative state simply by concentrating. In all these techniques, we take in the visual image through the method of single-pointed concentration. Techniques vary, but often it is helpful to keep our eyes partially open, gazing consistently at the object until they get heavy. Then we can close our eyes, keeping the image active in our imagination. When the inner image begins to fade, we can open our eyes again to gaze once more at the object of concentration.

In contrast to visual meditation experiences, when the object is often relatively static, in *kinesthetic* meditation the object of concentration is essentially dynamic. Many Eastern meditations follow kinesthetic methods. In Zen Buddhism, for example, the practice of *zazen* is characterized by concentration on the natural rhythms of breathing. For beginners, a teacher may give an instruction to count each inhalation and exhalation up to the number ten, then start over with the counting. At a more advanced level, practitioners may count only the exhalations. As the meditator progresses and is able to maintain awareness with less distraction, the counting is eliminated. So an advanced meditator is able to concentrate on the breathing alone. A deep awareness of one's inner body state arises. The pulsing of blood through the veins becomes a conscious experience. Or we may sometimes feel a gentle rocking as the body responds in tune with the pulsing heartbeat. It is as though we are resting in a boat, gently rocked by waves. The Tao of life flows through us. The body feels in tune with the rhythms of nature. The psyche calms itself as we rest in awareness of nature's rhythms.

Many Eastern forms of meditation have been transcribed into a Christian idiom in Anthony De Mello's book *Sadhana*. There he presents exercises that combine body sensations with visual imagination to provide opportunities for profound meditative experiences. Dance and the various martial arts of the Orient can also provide avenues for profound movement meditations. Another simple, but difficult to sustain, form of kinesthetic meditation is a kind of dynamic awareness called "mindfulness." (The same meditation was known as "recollection" in Christian tradition.) Staying simply aware of what happens in the here-and-now moment is the essence of mindfulness.

In Buddhist tradition, meditation techniques fall into two categories: "concentration" and "insight." In *concentration* practices, we emphasize the development of *one-pointed attention* to a single object, sound, or body rhythm. Eventually this concentration practice produces feelings of tranquility, contentment, and bliss, leading to states of absorption or trance. *Insight* practices, on the other hand, depend more on our ongoing attention, mindfulness, moment-to-moment awareness of the changing quality of our perceptions. In this practice, we develop attention to our momentary thoughts, feelings, images, and sensations. We become aware of all the phenomena going on around and within us. With practice we can observe even consciousness itself, as an *endless fluctuation, natural to all the mind and body processes.* A series of insights into the temporary, unstable, and impersonal nature of our own personalities are likely to occur. Travelers on this path of insight meditation may come eventually to the culminating experience that the Buddhists call enlightenment.

As we move into mindfulness, we also begin to get a sense of what the medieval mystic Brother Lawrence called "the practice of the presence of God." At this point, we have crossed over into contemplative experience. This awesome domain of "enlightenment" is the area we now approach.

Contemplation

After going over one of his very significant dreams, an undergraduate told me about a deep mystical experience he had received on awakening. "There was this image of Christ that simply stayed with me," he said. "I was surrounded by ancient texts from all around the world: Peru, the Philippines, Iran, France, and Denmark. I had such a sense that the wisdom of *all* the ancient books pointed to, or centered on, the figure of Christ. I felt so deeply moved to have seen this vision and

privileged beyond anything I could possibly deserve." Such a beautiful
experience is sufficient to sustain this young man's faith throughout his
lifetime.

A surprisingly large number of the American population (roughly
40 percent) admit to occasional forms of some mystical experience, yet
we tend not to talk of such things. For those who search for a spiritual dimension within themselves, contemplation is a very important
inner reality to consider. The contemplative experience is essentially
ineffable. Even the great mystics admit they can only partially describe
what happens to them inwardly. Descriptions can be merely suggestive
of the power and beauty of the encounter with ultimate reality. One
dictionary definition of contemplation is "to view thoughtfully." In this
regard, you can imagine standing in silence beholding the vista of a
starry night or gazing quietly at the sunrise radiating throughout the
Grand Canyon.

Many mystical writers have described their contemplative experiences using the metaphor of light. Sometimes light permeates the
mystic's inward gaze or, more at a beginner's level, the quality of light
may transform an ordinary scene into a deep awareness of the sacred permeating life. In contemplation, we may gaze at a panoramic
view, such as vast fields of growing grain, and the feeling becomes one
of wordless wonder. We are lifted beyond ourselves and we receive a
glimpse of something expansive, infinite, and magnificent. We perceive
how small we are in relation to the Divine. For a moment at least,
we lose our self-importance, and we become simple in our experience
of awe.

Simplicity and *silence* are two characteristics of contemplation. When
we become lost in wordless wonder, whatever the object of our contemplation, we are lifted up into a transcendent experience. These feelings
are beyond the ordinary. We have a sense of the incredible beauty and
rightness of life. We feel that somehow we are touched in a very special way. We feel an expansive Love, and we know it is somehow an
encounter with the Divine.

Since William James described the varieties of religious experience
at the turn of the twentieth century, we have been aware that contemplation, although relatively rare, is certainly accessible to many
ordinary people. It is sometimes difficult to discern genuine contemplative states. I recall being told of a dream of a simple cabbage. That
was it: layer upon layer of leaves simply unfolding. But the dreamer had

such a sense of numinosity and awe that we realized it was a sacred dream. The message seemed to be a call to be aware of "the sacred in the ordinary."

Such contemplative states seem to occur quite naturally in certain people. Those who have an introverted, intuitive nature may be more open to perceiving the touch of the Divine in ordinary experience. Some describe it as a sense of presence, closeness, and warmth. These feelings can occur even in the midst of hardship. For example, Harold dreamed of being cradled in the arms of a Divine Mother, just at a time when his job was threatened and he was faced with having to make major career changes. The appearance of deep spiritual awareness, whether in waking states or dreams, can be tremendously uplifting for people who are undergoing particularly difficult trials and stresses. It seems that those people who are comfortable with being passive may also have greater opportunities than other, more active people for this type of spiritual experience.

I once saw a nun in therapy who was from a contemplative religious order. She was unhappy because her spiritual life was not very deep. She knew the reason for the dryness in her prayer life: She was too busy to pray! She was active by nature and was too busy teaching and giving workshops on the contemplative life to find time to pray herself. Those of us who are very active by nature have to work hard to undo that active mode. Simplicity and silence are necessary. We must "not do" in order to receive the special graced moments of contemplation.

So many people are thirsty for something spiritual in their lives, but it seems to me that contemplation is not something we can strive to achieve directly; rather, we are occasionally lifted into this state when we persevere in prayer and/or meditation. The contemplative state is something similar to the meditative mood, but it seems to have greater uplift and it is more intense. True contemplation is a state in which we have at least a beginning sense of what union with the Divine may be. Especially for people who are close to death, such contemplative experiences may bring great consolation and blessing. Those who are suffering from AIDS, for example, have been reporting much deeper spiritual insights, often crossing over into contemplative experience.

Spiritual teachers know that at best it is futile, even counterproductive, to strive for contemplation. In other words, *it is pointless to work hard* to achieve such an altered state of mind. Nonetheless, contemplative experience is a goal for many who value the spiritual life. Many spiritually oriented people seem to harbor the secret wish to know God. For such people the desire to experience Divine Reality is most important, and they genuinely reverberate with that inner yearning.

As we know, there are very many different approaches to the spiritual life and each may evoke strong reactions, either positive or negative. Generally negative reactions come from people who have no experience of a particular spiritual approach. Today, in our pluralistic society there are many valid spiritual traditions, including Hindu, Buddhist, Sufi, and American Indian forms of spirituality. In general, "New Age" thinking tends to value a potpourri of these ideas, but be aware that what has "no meaning" for some people has "infinite meaning" for others. Throughout this book, my aim is to expose you to options you may not have considered. Spiritual folks who have advanced far along the mystical path are known to be extraordinary in their ability to cope effectively with life, just as it is.

To aid us in understanding the spiritual quest, there is an abundance of writings from both past and present eras that outline the history of spirituality and mysticism. While it is not my purpose to go into that literature in any depth, we can gain many useful insights from those who have described the life of grace. The mystical path is divided variously into stages. Many writers describe the three distinctive phases of purgation, illumination, and union. In *Purgation*, we are psychologically made ready for mystical experience by the increasing awareness of who we are as imperfect people. Gradually, we let our defenses down and we become aware of our patterns of dysfunction in relationships with others and of the many ways — both large and small — that we habitually attempt to fool ourselves and others. This awareness of our imperfection leads to positive changes in behavior.

In the second state, *Illumination*, the seeker begins to see patterns and the mystery in the world around. There is a sense that "this is the way the world is, and somehow it all works out as it should." An appreciation for divine kindness and loving care accompanies this phase. The image of the laughing Buddha suggests that joy and a sense of humor are natural components of what the Oriental mystics call enlightenment.

The stage of *Union* is one that the mystics from all traditions agree is an advanced state — some say the ultimate goal and resting place of the spiritual life. Union with the Divine Presence is at first tentative and temporary. The writings of many great mystics, however, suggest that abiding in that unitive state is not only humanly possible but is the ultimate, most worthwhile aim in life. Increasingly in our postmodern world, we are becoming aware of our need to take a unitive, global perspective. If we are to avoid blowing ourselves up or polluting ourselves out of existence, we may desperately need to look toward unification on all levels: spiritual as well as economic and political.

One spiritual leader who had a particular gift for synthesizing wisdom from the many religious traditions around the world was the Indian Jesuit Anthony De Mello. In his workshops and writings, he borrowed from Buddhist, Hindu, Sufi, and Christian traditions as well as from the work of numerous schools of American psychotherapy. "Wake up!" was his challenge. To become *aware* of the sensations in the physical world, both surrounding and within us, is the primary aim of De Mello-style spirituality. De Mello used Sufi tales and Zen koans as exercises for reflective thought and Tibetan Buddhist and Hindu breathing exercises as meditative underpinnings for Christian spiritual imagery. The sensate and the imaginal processes are combined in a potpourri of methods for evoking encounter with the divine life within. Those who follow De Mello's particularly creative process find deepening and enriching experiences at every unexpected turn.

De Mello revels in the unexpected. When we are fully aware, we relish every moment. "If you are not happy every single moment," says De Mello, "then there is something wrong with you!" So here is a spiritual leader who dares to hold out the radical hope that life can be truly joyous throughout.

One central secret to releasing our tensions and anxiety lies in the ability to detach from our personal wishes and desires. This is the Buddha's secret to happiness. As De Mello tells his followers, we hold ourselves in bondage as long as we allow the praise or criticism of others to determine our lives. If we give others the power to lift us up through their praise and admiration, we have also given over to them the power to shatter our tenuous self-esteem. De Mello asks: Will you let others destroy your self-esteem and your happiness by their criticism? Do you really want to give away that much power? Do you want to strive and suffer your whole life in an endless effort to please others? Each of us must find self-acceptance, and spiritually minded people find it most readily when they experience the Love of God within. De Mello reminds us, as a way out of our usual people-pleasing mode, that we already are who we are meant to be. This implies radical self-acceptance, which is inherent in the experience of the Divine within. The immanence of the godhead, recognizing God within, is proclaimed in the Buddhist phrase: "That thou art!" In this way spiritual life becomes an endless celebration, as we grow in deepening awareness of ourselves and of the truly marvelous workings of the world around us.

Clearly, this view of the world as full of peace, love, and joy is tremendously appealing. The promise of a joyful life is the primary magnetic aspect of the spiritual path. Both cynics and social scientists are quick to remind us, however, that most of the world does *not* experience endless happiness in daily life; far from it. We cannot help but wonder about the secrets of the spiritual path and about the ways in which this positive energy can be harnessed both to cope with difficulties and to make the world a better place in which humanity can survive.

If you have become a spiritual seeker, you may want to learn as much as you can about many spiritual traditions. But then I suggest you choose *one* path and follow it. Follow it faithfully, going as far as you are able. Let your spiritual path simplify and focus your life. The energy of love naturally arises. Let it change your life, heal your relationships, bring you closer and closer to your own perception of God. The meaning of life will deepen. Go as far as you are able, but don't get caught in a futile search for psychical or magical powers. That's not the end result you seek.

As you grow older, your desire for a spiritual way of life will probably deepen. Despite the physical limitations of old age, some capacities you will always have are prayer, meditation, and the contemplative life. The spiritual way will provide inner peace, helping you to cope with all the trials you must face.

Take, for example, this very moment. Out of the rich array of possibilities open to you right now, focus on this moment and, in trust, look about you to find the sacred in the ordinary. Most spiritual paths ultimately come to this appreciation. In any one moment, millions (no trillions, quadrillions) of events are happening throughout the world. A child is born, someone becomes lame, an old man dies, a woman is baking bread, a boy learns to read, a dog is playing with a little girl. In any one moment all those things are happening out there. But even right here, even as you look up from this book, in any one moment thousands of perceptions are available for your appreciation. You might notice, as I do, the light glistening on raindrops outside the window. What do you see that is both sacred and ordinary? Notice it in detail. Be aware. Let it carry you to a deep inner place of appreciation and love. In this moment of full awareness and presence, you touch the Divine. Your life is uplifted.

Spirituality for Coping

For each of us, in our personal lives, when we take the bird's eye view of the spiritual stream and look at the variety of spiritual methods that are available for coping, we need to pose three questions: (1) How can spirituality help in our daily lives? (2) How does it help in extraordinary times? (3) How does spirituality provide assistance in the long-term adjustments such as those that arise in the context of chronic illness?

In *daily life*, spirituality serves psychologically as a preventive coping method. The little hassles and stresses have less impact when we are spiritually oriented. When we "practice the presence of God," we are more serene, and ordinary frustrations are less likely to be upsetting. Although we all feel stressed and upset from time to time, there is research evidence to show that meditators and those who pray on a frequent basis tend to have more rapid return to a sense of inner balance and harmony. This sense of inner harmony affects us in a complete, holistic way. Whenever we do our spiritual practice, we relax and the parasympathetic nervous system brings us back to harmony, calming us both physiologically and mentally. We're much less likely to encounter the "overload" feeling. We are more placid and, therefore, more effective both in the work we do and in our relations.

At times of *extraordinary* stress, we all tend to reach out somewhat desperately. We turn then to our strongest resources. Religious people pray both for themselves and for their loved ones. When we feel powerless in the face of a major crisis, we call out in supplication to whatever Deity we can envision. Even people who are essentially nonreligious, or have given up their institutional affiliations, tend to turn to a Divine Being at times of crisis. One elderly man prayed simply and eloquently when his son had an alcohol-related accident. This father sat in his rocking chair, looked at his son and then turned his eyes heavenward. He prayed simply: "Big Fella, help me!" Simple prayer is sometimes the most meaningful. Heartfelt prayer speaks volumes, sometimes in very few words.

Times of illness and injury are those times when we are most likely to evoke our spiritual resources. When we feel powerless, we turn most readily to God. We surrender our illusory efforts at control. We acknowledge our limitations and we seek fortitude, comfort, consolation, and healing. Sorrow brings us figuratively to our knees. So does fear. Illness and injury impact us sometimes at the very core of our selves.

When I worked in rehabilitation, I saw those many families who were coping with the results of accidents and neurological diseases. Time and again, the medical team worked extraordinarily hard to help the patient regain as much of the lost functions as possible. They worked until the patient reached a plateau. Then, when there was no more improvement, they sent the patient home. Billy, for example, was brain-injured. He progressed in rehab until he could walk and talk again. His thinking capacity was still intact, but his memory was gone. A twenty-year-old with no memory! He was discharged to his parents' care. Time and again, I saw families such as this one turning to prayer. They prayed while their loved ones struggled in physical therapy. They prayed for strength for themselves. They prayed for acceptance so that both they and the patient would be able to go on without suffering the debilitating effects of depression. They prayed for sustenance in the long months ahead when the patient would be home, often having to cope with a serious disability. And then, in their generosity, they prayed for one another. Prayer served as a bond among the suffering people. Sometimes they would tell me in private: "I prayed for that old lady down the hall. She's having such a rough time." In their prayer, they felt an uplift and renewed hope. In prayer, they found the courage to go on.

Courage is needed in so many of life's situations. Imagine the challenge eighteen-year-old Evelyn faced when her bicycle hit a small rock and sent her careening off into space. When she awoke, her spinal cord was severed. She was alive, but she would never walk again. Such challenges we must courageously face whenever there has been a serious accident. You or your loved one may have to cope with such a stable disability, perhaps life in a wheelchair. Evelyn counsels others now. She taught me that the first step in adaptation happens when you acknowledge the fact that you need to change your lifestyle. Then your adjustment to the limiting disability may take months or even years. Eventually, you find a new form of inner balance. When you can achieve inner harmony, you will find that renewed *hope* is possible. You may no longer hope for complete recovery; you know it is unrealistic to hope for return of the lost limb or regaining of the lost functions, but you find renewed hope and motivation for *other* forms of growth, nourishment, achievement, and gratification.

Terry taught me that there is a difference between adapting to a relatively stable disability and adjusting to a chronic illness. If your situation is one of *long-term* debilitating illness, the challenges you face are ongoing. Chronic illness is often not stable, and sometimes you must expect and prepare for a deteriorating course. The courage to cope with slow physical deterioration will require both mental fortitude and spiritual grace. When a realistic assessment of the situation suggests reason for despair, how do you cope and keep your spirits alive? Terry found that, for him, being on a spiritual path and teaching others how to meditate brought the most hope and reward and sense of meaning to life.

While some depression is inevitable in situations of chronic illness, despondency does not have to be long-lasting. Those people who are able to call on their spiritual resources suffer less depression in the face of illness and impending death than other, less spiritually minded people do. As Eugene Bianchi tells us in his book *Aging as a Spiritual Journey*, the spiritual road does not seek to avoid major problems, but rather enters into them with full understanding. The Tao flows not away from, not in avoidance, but *through* the pain and loss of life.

The spiritual life teaches us about the value to be found in accepting our losses. Spiritual renouncement has been a mystical ideal in every major religious tradition. To practice renouncement, we need not necessarily *seek* opportunities to relinquish our desires, for life itself continually demands sacrifice from us. Whether it is the death of a child or the loss of a limb that must be amputated, we cannot grasp that which can no longer be ours. The question is, how do we let go? The psychospiritual process of surrender requires both discipline and grace.

In Al-Anon, the fellowship of relatives of alcoholics, they so frequently say: "Let go and let God." Letting go means the surrender of our habitual inclinations to control everything. In letting go, we surrender both our ego control and our own desire. In giving up control, we surrender these desires into the hands of an Almighty One. The grace that follows comes from the recognition that a power greater than ourselves is guiding this universe. Life evolves according to pattern, and we are but a small part of it all.

A spiritual orientation also allows us to see life from a different, broader perspective. Our individual trials are less overwhelming when we see them in the context of the vast suffering of all humanity. We know the universal human condition is to suffer periodically. But how does that knowledge help us to cope?

Victor Frankl, after years of reflecting on the tragic suffering of Jews during the Holocaust, concluded that our search for a meaning is the surest sign of true humanity. He found at all levels of life experience, including pain and horrendous times of deprivation, human beings search for meaning and value. Those who are able to grope for meaning in the midst of painful existence are motivated, not only to survive, but also to find glimpses of the sacred in life just as it is.

In the veterans hospital where I used to work, the guard at the swimming pool entrance was a cheerful Jamaican. He loved to tease both patients and staff members alike. When his eyes would start to sparkle, you could always predict that soon his round black face would open up to show his gleaming white grin. One day I stopped to talk to Ed, as I was curious about how he managed to have such an ever-ready smile. He told me he gets a lot of enjoyment out of cheering up the patients who were so much worse off than he. "The staff too," he said, "their jobs are mostly a lot tougher than mine." Ed's job in his eyes was to lighten up the atmosphere. That was one part of the meaning he found in life. Ed's other dedication was to his family at home. He had a son with muscular dystrophy and a young daughter also in his care. "My wife died ten years ago," he said. "I could get remarried, I suppose. That might be nice, but I gotta take care of them kids at home. They're what keep me going. Lots of single people go out and have a ball. Not me. I get me right home whenever I can and see them kids of mine." Life wasn't easy, but Ed was always very clear what he was about.

Those who have studied coping know that altruism is an important aspect of finding meaning in life. Altruism increases self-esteem, and it connects us to the rest of the human race. In the human condition, all of us suffer. To be altruistic we need to have compassion for the suffering of others. When we have a sense of meaning in life, it puts our own suffering in perspective.

From the spiritual perspective, superficial things lose their significance. You gain an increased sense of the importance of those things that really matter. For Roberto, who knows he will die soon, relationships take on new meaning. Ultimate things matter more. Love is central. Courage is vital. He said, "You find yourself reordering your priorities and rediscovering faith in the essential strength of the human spirit."

In the spiritual life, in order to master our human tendencies to despair, we each need to make the courageous struggle with all the sorrow and frustration of our human condition. Mastering despair means entering into our own emptiness, accepting the inward darkness. Going through the dark places with conscious awareness allows us to progress again into the light. Like the spiritual path described by the mystics, encountering the Void requires letting go. When we surrender and do not run away, as we may at first be inclined to do, we ultimately have available to us the resources of mystical experience. Each of us can discover the inner rebirth and feel renewed. Then we feel again the grace, the joy, and the hope. We know that we are loved and supported in our every movement. In each renewal we come to the vital appreciation of life; we recognize that in spite of our faults we are worthwhile, and we experience again how precious relationships truly are. We know in a deeper way the meaning of love. In this central experience we encounter, in all its simplicity, the core of life.

5

Knowing Your Body's Ways

❖

I N THE TAO OF COPING, the Body's ways provide practical down-to-earth wisdom for what we can and cannot do. Body's ways are full of mystery: What wondrous changes happen in the body? What transformations of matter and energy? Whatever its current state of health, this body is our home. Our skin is the boundary of our separate personhood. Reality begins and ends here. How can we be so naive that we misuse this precious instrument or take it for granted? Incomprehensible as it may seem, we frequently forget the needs of body in the press of daily life. Yet, our bodies are intricately balanced systems. Each body needs to be worked, to be stimulated, and to be rested. The rhythms of our lives require daily balance and harmony. In this chapter, we reflect on the body and the ways we can optimize our physical health so that we can cope most effectively.

Awareness

A multiple sclerosis patient writes: "When I was diagnosed at the age of twenty-eight, my neurologist suggested three things to live with MS: lessen the amount of animal fat in my diet, rest when I am tired, and do what makes me happy, three seemingly simple tasks. For me, resting when fatigued has been the most difficult to achieve. I often tend to push myself too long and too far. One thing that helps me to cope is listening to what my body is telling me.

"I have always loved sports and for a while I was able to continue to play on a softball team. I found I played as well as ever at that time, but I would get exhausted long before others did. I'd go home after a game and sleep for ten hours straight. Now, I keep my exercise to walking. I'm slower now, but I try to walk at least two or three miles every other day. And I don't go out when the weather is too hot. I have learned to admit it when I can't do something. I've learned that I don't need to

108

feel like a failure and I've learned not to think that MS is preventing me from living. I don't stay up late anymore, and I don't insist on doing things that I can't because that only leaves me with a sense of defeat. Sometimes I have more energy than at other times, and I've learned to let my friends and family know what my current limitations are. I've gotten to be pretty observant of my energy level, so I'm getting a lot better at judging how much I can do."

In listening to your body, it is helpful to ask first: What does your body need? If you feel a twinge, stay with that awareness. What is it saying? Is there fatigue? Tension? A need to express some emotion? To cooperate with the body, we need to listen as it communicates its feelings: pain, pleasure, and emotions. By learning to listen to our bodies, we open ourselves to a vast storehouse of knowledge. By listening to the metaphoric language of our symptoms and discomforts, we can often relieve the immediate physiological distress, and we can also learn to tap into the wisdom of the psychosomatic whole of the organism.

What happens when you try breathing deeply, relaxing and letting your awareness slowly drift across your entire body? This type of exercise allows you to befriend your body so that it will guide you and will help increase your comfort (see Appendix A, Exercise 2, p. 192). *Awareness* is the key to knowing what you need. For example, when you become fully aware of a tension, you often almost automatically find the way that will best serve to release that excess energy. Often a bit of stretching will allow you to regain a sense of comfort. Some of the other proven ways to discharge excess energy are: shaking, crying, sexual orgasm, pounding, kicking, stretching, and yawning. These are natural mechanisms that restore a sense of harmony and a feeling of well-being. All sorts of aerobic exercises, which include running, tennis, swimming, dancing, bicycling, racquetball, and team sports, are also good tension releasers. When you discharge excess energy, you are using natural physical means to relieve the negative effects of stress on your body.

When we think about the natural functions of yawning, shaking, and crying, we realize that all three are often judged socially unacceptable, and yet each of these actions can be wonderful for discharging negative energy. *Yawning* allows you to increase oxygen throughout your entire bloodstream because you breathe in huge quantities of fresh air and expel carbon dioxide. When you are anxious, you tend to constrict your breathing. Anxiety makes you hold your chest tight, preventing full inhalation or exhalation. We know that yoga breathing exercises are designed to counteract the constricted airflow associated with anxiety, but did you realize that yawning accomplishes the same thing quickly and naturally?

Crying is a more popular form of tension release. Women have traditionally been freer to give in to the wonderful release of crying. But recently men, too, have begun to learn how to cry. All it takes is giving yourself permission to use this natural function. Research has shown that tears contain chemicals and part of the relief after a "good cry" is due to the discharge of these slightly toxic wastes. We all know that tears are the natural discharge for grief and depression. We can also relieve frustration and anger by allowing the spontaneous outpouring of tears. When heavy sobbing accompanies our tears, we naturally get additional physical release. We surrender our muscle tension and this release gives us the general psychological sense of "letting go."

Many people do not realize it, but *shaking* is an equally beneficial natural release. Harvey Jackins studied the various human and animal discharge functions and noticed that automatic shaking occurs when we are intensely frightened. He went on to discover that we can relieve our fears — even paralyzing fears — when we consciously begin the process of shaking. For example, a young woman came for therapy, suffering from panic attacks. She had been raped in an alley behind a shopping mall. Every time she went shopping, her feelings of panic ensued. We worked on many aspects of her fears, talking through her memories of the trauma. But she still had that stone wall of fear whenever she approached any shopping mall. We worked on a gradual approach. As she got closer to places and people that frightened her, she would give herself permission to retreat to the ladies' room or back to her car. There in privacy, she let herself shake out the fear — shake her hands, shake her legs, shake all over until the fear abated. She said, "When you shake hard it's like you shake out the fear itself."

Body Needs

A person who is completely human, healthy, and alive enters each moment of life fully aware, giving his or her wholehearted participation. Hearty living seems to be highly correlated with longevity. To live fully, you must keep your body in optimal condition for work and play. Your body, like any machine, requires certain "inputs" to keep it working well. As we know, these include proper diet, sufficient sleep, exercise, and breath.

Diet and Nutrition. Many books and pamphlets are available on the subject of diet, nutrition, and control of weight. Unfortunately, they sometimes give conflicting advice. Considering the psychological aspects of coping with our need for food should be beneficial. As adults, we can learn to listen to our bodies in mature ways by questioning ourselves: Is this really hunger I feel? Or is it partly emotional overload? Do I need food? Or is it perhaps rest or exercise I need? If it is, in fact, food that I need, then I must ask, not just what would appeal right now, but what will make my body function well. We can safely say that some foods (for example, fatty, sugary, "junk" food or other "rich" foods) should be avoided by most people, most of the time (the exception being anorexics who need to gain essential weight). We also know that food allergies may develop at any time during adulthood, so with any change in digestive patterns, one should consider the possible need to restrict one's diet further. For most of us, however, the American Cancer Society and the American Heart Association have good suggestions for healthy eating in adulthood. They also recommend drinking plain water (iced in the summer and hot in the winter) or light herb teas. Clearly what we need is a new way to think about eating. An approach based on moderation, sound nutrition, self-acceptance, personal harmony, and exercise is most likely to promote good long-term health habits and a sense of fulfillment in living.

Sleep. In addition to problems of weight control, bad sleep habits may plague the older population. We often adopt our sleep patterns during adolescence and young adulthood, but sleep abnormalities may ensue. Insomnia at night and daytime drowsiness may be the long-term result of irregular sleep patterns in youth. Then too, menopause may lead to sleep disturbance in women, due to fluctuating biochemistry in the wake of estrogen loss.

In order to prevent or to reduce sleep disorders, sleep specialists recommend that we maintain regularity in our sleep-wake cycle. Shift workers who must stay up at night and travelers who are subject to time zone shifts and "jet lag" are particularly vulnerable to developing sleep problems. The specialists recommend a regular time for arising and a reasonable time for going to bed. This provides a sense of balance and harmony, which are the positive result of regularity in our daily rhythms.

At times of peak stress, sleep is often disturbed. Sometimes you may awake with a troubling dream. The pounding of your heart in the middle of the night announces your sympathetic nervous system has gone into fight-or-flight mode and your adrenaline has begun to flow. Often, it may be hours before you can get back to sleep. It is not a good idea to lie in bed worrying about your problems at such times. A glass of milk can be soothing and may help you get back to sleep. You may find that sleep comes more easily if you read for a while and/or practice self-hypnosis to induce sleep. Meditation, particularly those forms that leave the mind blank, can be a beneficial way to cope with insomnia and to promote the onset of sleep. Any of the breathing or relaxation activities that I describe below can also be useful. Especially when you are facing heavy stress, you can cope most effectively by maintaining (or trying to quickly regain) a state of balance for both your mind and body.

Relaxation

In her popular book *Minding the Body, Mending the Mind,* Joan Borysenko describes a number of scientifically sound methods to elicit what she calls the relaxation response. She speaks for many experts in the field when she writes of our need for a synthesis of mental and physical exercises to counteract the potentially killing effects of stress and pressures in our society. We desperately need to learn to relax, to comfort the body, and reduce its physiological response to stress.

An important psychological aspect of the relaxation response entails taming the mind. As I discussed in chapter 4, meditation has both physical and spiritual benefits. For example, Borysenko describes mindfulness as meditation in action, that is, a "be here now" approach that allows us to perceive life as it unfolds without limiting what we perceive by our expectations. Mindfulness involves opening to the moment, relaxing like a child who is deeply intent on play. The mindful state is totally involved in the enjoyment of doing the ordinary things of life.

A second important component of relaxation is complete breathing. The first step is to become aware of your normal, habitual breathing patterns. A few minutes of mindful breathing can provide a soothing respite and stress reducer. Then even two or three deeper breaths can make a difference in a busy day. A more complete breathing exercise comes from the methods of Hatha (physical) yoga. Pranayama means rhythmic control of the breath, and the complete, three-part breath is a rolling motion that soothes while it provides a cleansing of all the inner airways. In this exercise air expands first the abdomen, then the rib cage, then the upper chest (see Appendix A, Exercise 3, p. 194). It's good to practice about six complete, three-part breaths several times a day. This breathing exercise is useful before periods of meditation or when you are especially challenged and need to think clearly and perform well.

In addition to mindfulness and breathing, exercising your body is the third major way for releasing tension and allowing relaxation to occur. Aerobic exercises that are rapid provide a thorough workout for your heart and lungs, if your physical health permits. Usually, a very pleasant state of relaxation follows a period of such active exercise. (Note that your sleep may be delayed following aerobic exercise, however, so aerobics are not recommended for the late evening hours.)

Another entirely different form of exercise has become popular in recent years. These are the yoga stretching exercises from the Hindu tradition of the East. One particularly good, brief yogic exercise for release of tension and increased suppleness is "The Salute to the Sun," to be practiced at least twice each morning on arising (see Appendix A, Exercise 4, p. 194).

In the last two decades, we have seen an explosion of clinical experimentation, developing new methods to help the American population learn how to relax. One of the best books, *The Relaxation Response,* was written by Harvard Medical School cardiologist Herbert Benson, who points out that learning to relax can be lifesaving, particularly for patients who have suffered such life-threatening afflictions as heart attacks and strokes. Diet, exercise, and meditation are all vital elements in a cardiac survival plan.

Physicians and other medical specialists have turned to psychologists for their expertise in relaxation training. The method Edmund Jacobson developed in 1938 is still the leading technique. Using the Jacobsonian method, you learn to relax by first tensing each of the muscle groups, then releasing the tension and noticing how different your body feels. After you work through each of the muscle groups (hands, arms, face, neck, shoulder blades and upper chest, buttocks and abdomen, feet and legs) tensing and releasing, you complete the relaxation with a few deep breaths (see Appendix A, Exercise 5, p. 195).

It is now generally well recognized that stress can have negative effects on health and that relaxation is valuable to counteract the stress. What many people do not understand, however, is how the different states of body and mind interact. We can learn from the stress researchers how we trigger the specific physiological mechanisms in response to stressful events. Awareness of these processes helps us to realize how important it is to monitor our stress level, how important it is to provide relaxation as a buffer against stress, and how essential it is to attend to our body's needs so that we can cope with the unavoidable stresses, without becoming emotionally unbalanced or physically ill.

Stress Has Effects on Your Body

A security guard sat on his stool, calmly reading his newspaper across from the Bronx Zoo. It was a beautiful evening full of late summer softness, the trees still green and the sky tinged with pink. He was laid back, with his feet propped up as he scanned the evening news.

Suddenly a rifle shot! A scream pierced the evening quiet. Four more shots and the sound of tires screeching as a car sped away. The victim lay on the ground, not twenty feet from where the guard sat. He ran to her and took her pulse. Yes, she was still breathing. He saw the agony of her pain, felt her blood sticky on his hands. He knew he would have to move quickly. Totally alert, he moved to the phone in his guard booth. Call the police, call the ambulance, let his supervisor know. They'd send help as soon as his calls got through. The wail of the sirens arriving fast. The flashing lights, red and white. Move to comfort her. Help the technicians move her. Report what he saw.

Some jobs are inherently stressful. Emergencies call forth adrenaline. The body instantly moves into "fight or flight" mode. A thousand stimuli impinge on the body. Stress is a physiological response. (Were you aware of a shift in your own body as you read the last two paragraphs?) Hans Selye, discoverer of the stress effects on the body, writes about "The Stress Concept Today" in Kutash and Schlesinger's *Handbook on Stress and Anxiety:*

> Stress, like relativity, is a scientific concept which has suffered from the mixed blessing of being too well known and too little understood. We are exposed to stress every moment of our lives,

and our response to it often determines the quality of our life and health....

Stress is the nonspecific response of the body to any demand.... Heat, cold, joy, sorrow, muscular exertion, drugs, and hormones elicit highly specific responses.... All those agents, however, have one thing in common: they increase the demand for readjustment, for performance of adaptive functions which reestablish normalcy.

In the 1940s, when Selye was doing animal experiments, he found some remarkable parallels that led to his pioneering definition and description of the concept of stress. Selye discovered that animals react to *any* stimulus that has impact on their bodies with three common physiological changes. These characteristic changes are: (1) enlargement and hyperactivity of the adrenal cortex, (2) atrophy of the thymus and lymph nodes, and (3) gastrointestinal ulcers. Together these three reactions form a cluster of symptoms that Selye called the *General Adaptation Syndrome.*

Selye discovered that this syndrome occurs in three stages. The first stage, called the *Alarm Reaction,* occurs when the organism (human or animal) is exposed to any novel stimulus, that is, when the body must adapt to something new. The body immediately reacts with shock and countershock, that is, a rebound effect mobilizing the defenses. In this process, the adrenal gland enlarges and begins secreting corticoid hormones. Most acute stress diseases get their start at these two initial phases of the alarm reaction. Next follows a *Stage of Resistance.* By now the body is fully mobilized, adapting to the stress. The disease symptoms usually disappear at this point, but the body has less resistance to most *other* stimuli. The final stage of *Exhaustion* comes on if the stressor is sufficiently severe and prolonged. Even death may occur if the stress goes on unrelieved.

The important point is that the body's capacity to adjust, which Selye calls "adaptation energy," is finite. We can tolerate only so much exposure to stress. Fatigue usually reminds us to slow down, preventing us from being foolish and wasting our precious adaptation energy too lavishly. Sleep and rest can restore our resistance and adaptability time and time again, but eventually the machine breaks down. So, as Selye tells us, the human body sooner or later wears out as a result of constant wear and tear.

Medical and psychological research has since been aiming to understand the implications of Selye's findings. One avenue of research has been to explore the causative factors, that is, the *stressors*. There are three types: physical, social, and psychological. Physical stressors include noise, radiation, toxins, and all other concrete substances that may have impact on our bodies. Unless they are severe, we tend to adapt eventually to most physical stressors. Social stressors result from our interaction with other people or groups in our environment. Some events, such as the loss of someone we love, may have acute, damaging effects on us. Conflict with other people is another common source of stress. Systems in chaos are stressful for everyone. These social stressors are external and often at least partly beyond our control. Psychological stressors, on the other hand, happen within our psyches and involve all the internal emotions including frustration, anger, hate, jealousy, fear, anxiety, sorrow, self-pity, and inferiority feelings. Selye tells us that emotional arousal is one of the most frequent effects of stress and, if we feel chronic, intensely negative emotional states, they may be more damaging to our health than physical stressors. Emotional arousal itself is a form of stress. In this light, you can begin to see why meditation is so helpful, because it helps to reduce our arousal as rapidly as possible.

When you are stressed, your body tends to concentrate its energies, shutting off the energy flow to other bodily functions that are less immediately necessary for survival. Your sympathetic nervous system becomes active, releasing the stress hormones: adrenaline, noradrenalin, and cortisone. Your body is geared up to fight or to flee from the stressor. The physiological effects in the sympathetic nervous system response are manifold, affecting digestion, breath, blood chemistry and dynamics, nerves, muscles, glands, sensory organs, saliva, hormones, and responses to pain and infection. These effects of the sympathetic nervous system arousal are all geared to prepare your body for strenuous physical exertion, just as the security guard was mobilized, prepared almost immediately to respond when the sound of the shots activated his body.

In the days of our forebears, when human survival depended on being able to send an arrow to the heart or to escape from a bear in the woods, the sympathetic nervous system arousal had obvious meaning in terms of evolution and survival. In today's "civilized" environment, the survival value of such physiological arousal has changed. In fact, a driven, fast-paced personality (known as Type A) is *more likely to succumb* to heart attack and other stress-related diseases. Today's executives face stresses of a different sort. They are less likely to need physical strength and more in need of staying calm. Today, health and longevity depend more on the counteractive effect of the parasympathetic nervous system. This system shuts down the excessive arousal and returns the body to a state of balance.

The parasympathetic nervous system acts as a counterbalance to the arousal mechanisms of the sympathetic nervous system. The balance it aims for is known as homeostasis. You feel your body calming down and normalizing: slower heartbeat and breathing, improved blood circulation to your hands and feet, better digestion, and lower muscle tension are among the parasympathetic effects you feel. These effects are what you achieve when you practice relaxation, meditation, visualization, and trance.

In addition to learning relaxation techniques, a second way to help our bodies cope is to monitor and control the stress level in our environments. Although many stressors are uncontrollable, we do in fact have some control over the *pace of change* in our lives. Here is an example of how one family set their priorities. A forty-year-old professional man sought counseling when his wife died of breast cancer, leaving him with three small children. For the first few months after her death, he dealt with the largely unavoidable stresses: he had to cope with his own feelings of loss, the stress of her funeral, the seemingly endless paperwork and hassles in probate of the estate, managing their home, and arranging for childcare, which meant interviewing many people and beginning again whenever a nanny left, which frequently happened. All this was in addition to his usual business career. After six months, some friends introduced him to a widow who had two sons. He liked her and they dated. He decided she would be a good mother to his children and a good, loving support in his life, so within the year, he proposed and they decided to marry.

Now there were many choices for this couple to make. Should they live in his house or hers? How would their respective children adjust to a new school environment? Should they add on to the house? Or perhaps they should build a new house together? Maybe he should change his job so they could move to a different city where she had a good job offer? Questions of geographical location and lifestyle were significant for all members of this blending family. In addition, interactions with extended family on both sides led to the discovery of differing expectations and priorities.

As they discussed these decisions, both partners tried to express and clarify their values for themselves and for their families. They quickly learned that their stress level would need to be their overriding concern. "How much stress can we tolerate right now?" came to be a guiding factor in the decisions they made: They needed to *modulate the pace of change in order to keep the stress threshold low enough* so that all of them could cope effectively. Some things they postponed. Building a new house was not necessary right at the start. Nor was it a good idea for him to change his job right now. They began to focus together on ways they could plan their lives to minimize the number and intensity of changes that they had to make. Although the wedding itself and the blending of the two families created many, many tasks, and certain stresses were unavoidable, they began to feel more in control. They began to develop a sense of mastery and adjustment as they worked together to avoid or postpone those changes that were not absolutely necessary. Change per se is stressful. This family was wise enough to make conscious choices of how much they could handle. The father, in particular, had an overload of stress in the previous two years and he needed to pace himself in order to minimize the likelihood of becoming ill.

In their classic stress studies, researchers Holmes and Rahe found that there is a gradation of stressful effects that result from common life events. For example, these researches found that receiving a parking ticket or purchasing a new home are considered low and moderate levels of stress, respectively. In the Holmes and Rahe Life Change Events Scale, events are rated on the basis of the amount of adjustment they require. Having a severe illness in the family or going through a divorce are much more stressful events, and the most severely stressful is the death of a spouse.

The important point to recognize is that the stress from life change is *cumulative*. All change creates stress because change brings with it multitudes of new stimuli that require your system to adapt. Even positive change, such as a wedding, is a stressor. So you need to consider any change, whether positive or negative, in the equation when you are making choices about your timing and priorities. Recent research shows that positive or neutral events are less likely to produce negative health consequences. Nonetheless, change in itself is stressful, and it would be wise to keep in mind the overall amount of change you have had lately.

Stress and Illness

As Selye pointed out in his early research, the physiological effects of too much stress show up in changes in your body functioning, which can lead to a variety of illnesses. Recent biomedical research elucidates the many ways stress can lead to bodily dysfunction or illness, including neurological and psychiatric disorders, vascular conditions, migraine and cardiac disorders, elevated stress hormones from the hypothalamus in the brain and the adrenal gland, allergic reactions, and muscular spasms such as back pain. Our growing appreciation of the mind-body interaction has helped many people to gain understanding of their illnesses in the past few decades. Selye writes of these well recognized psychosomatic interactions:

> Every disease, of course, causes stress, since it imposes demands for adaptation upon the organism. In turn, stress plays some role in the development of every disease; its effects are added to the specific changes caused by the disease, and may be curative or damaging, depending on whether the stress reactions combat or accentuate the trouble.
>
> Unremitting stress can break down the body's protective mechanism.... Potentially pathogenic microbes are in or around us all the time; yet they cause no disease until we are exposed to stress. In this case, the illness is due neither to the microbe nor to stress but to the combined effect of both. In most instances, *disease is due neither to the germ as such nor to our adaptive reactions as such but to the inadequacy of our reactions against the germ.*

In the integrative field that is called "psychoneuroimmunology," researchers have come to recognize that the human organism, both mind and body, acts as a complex system. Each system within the organism interacts with every other system. This means that whatever psychological or social events you encounter in the world, as well as physical stimuli, will affect your body functioning; and vice versa, your body affects how you feel and behave with others. This interaction also means that all the physical systems within your body are interrelated. There

are many practical implications to these discoveries. When one system in your body is under stress or breaks down, other systems react
and respond. Sometimes healthy systems will carry the workload of the
damaged part, or sometimes the other systems will give way in a sort
of internal "domino effect."

Consider an athlete who has a knee injury. If he walks around for six
weeks with a brace and Ace bandages, it causes a shift in posture that
puts strain on his back. The first stress, the knee injury, puts demands
on another system, the back muscles. If they are weakened, the back
muscles may give out, resulting in lower back pain. The patient then
needs to work through a rehabilitation program in which he can learn
new exercises to cope with and recover from *both* injuries. In this way,
stressors disrupt our internal balance, or homeostasis, and require the
other systems in the body to adapt. Selye uses the image of a chain to
describe how the whole organism is under strain and the weakest link
is most likely to break down. The same stressor may affect different
people in different ways and, for each of us, the weakest link in our
physical body may be related to our genetic inheritance.

Another situation where we can clearly see the way systems within
the body interact occurs with cancer patients who have to undergo a
long series of treatments that may cause chain effects. The initial tu-
mor acts as a stressor on a specific area in the body. Treatment usually
begins when pain occurs or, better, when preventive diagnostic tests
spot the problem before the patient notices any pain. Global treatments
such as chemotherapy have direct effects on the patient's entire body.
Radiation has direct effects on a more limited area, and surgery may
be much more localized. All treatments have some effect, either direct or indirect, on the entire organism, however. So the treatments
themselves cause stress. Although the treatments are necessary, the
body has to work extra hard to regain its homeostatic balance. Relaxation and visualization exercises can be very helpful to encourage the
parasympathetic system to regain its balance.

The endocrine and immune systems are two of the ways in which
many parts of the body are connected. The immune system fights infection and the endocrine system keeps all the hormones in balance,
both very important for seriously ill patients. For cancer patients, when
chemotherapy lowers the immune system, there may be susceptibility
to secondary infection, and there is sometimes a sense of one thing
seeming to break down after another. These secondary effects can cre-

ate a chain of events that require additional coping on the part of the patient. This is called "cluster stress."

The nature of a system is such that when one part is changed, all other parts must change in relation to it. Just as stress in one part of the body tends to lead to stress in other parts as well, so also with positive events. When we use visualization and relaxation exercises to change the body in a positive, restful, healing manner, we relieve the stress in each of the parts. Just as the "domino effect" can lead to one part breaking down after another, so also a calming, coping effect can lead to gradual improvement in the physical health of the whole organism. Health in one part of the system leads to better functioning of the whole. This is why it is so important to maintain our sense of balance or to quickly regain that homeostatic balance whenever stress has knocked us "off kilter."

Bernie Siegel takes advantage of the psyche-soma interaction when he uses both psychological and physical methods for diagnosis and treatment of cancer patients. He describes how he asks his patients to draw themselves, to draw their treatment, and then to draw their disease. He then asks them to draw their white cells eliminating the disease. Siegel finds that talking about the treatment and use of visualization can change attitudes and lead to successful therapy. He calls this "reprogramming at an unconscious level."

When Selye developed the concept of stress, he opened the door for the very useful understanding we have gained about how mind and body interact. Not only have we come to realize how psychological events affect the body, but also great advances in medical science have come about as a result of the new understanding of the interrelatedness of the physical systems. We now know that stress plays a very significant role both in the onset of illness and in flare-ups that may occur later on. This is not by any means a simple relationship and involves a multitude of factors. Some factors to consider include social conditions both before and during the person's exposure to stress, how long the person has been under stress, and how responsive the person is, that is, the capacity to cope. In order to predict disease susceptibility, we would also need to consider other physical factors including genetic predisposition to certain traits (the weak link), sex, age, habits, early experience, diet, drugs, hormones, and external physical surroundings. This full array of interacting factors ultimately determines who will get sick and who will remain healthy.

Stress and Health

There is no doubt that the amount and type of stress we experience impact our physical bodies and our subjective sense of well-being. However, we have become increasingly aware that we cannot survive without some stress in our lives. To keep the body in optimal condition for work and play, we need a certain amount of stimulation and exercise. How much stress we need or can tolerate at any one time depends on our general stress threshold level. We can be overstressed, which can lead to illness, or we can be understressed, in which case life appears to be boring and we feel uninvolved. Human beings naturally need goals toward which we can work.

Through our efforts, we become fit and we attune ourselves to our surrounding social environment. We need to be sufficiently self-aware to find our own natural stress level and we need to give ourselves permission to cut back on activities when we reach the threshold point of "stress overload." People differ, so this optimum level of stress and the threshold level of overstress, vary from one person to the next. The optimum amount of stress may also differ for the same person from one time to another. The optimal range of stress for any one person is influenced by several things, including heredity and the person's perception of what others expect.

To cope creatively with the stresses in your life, you need to follow your own natural interests and to be attuned to your own self, recognizing what you need both physically and psychologically. When you can seek out and store up enough supplies of respect, self-esteem, support, and love from others, you will be less worried about pleasing everyone else and less likely to overwork yourself beyond your limits. Selye concludes that it is not the specific stress that we face but how well we face it that counts. How we cope affects how detrimental or beneficial stress is in our lives. Certainly we have little influence over some of the internal and external events that we face, but we do have at least limited control over our lives. How well we exercise this control can determine whether we are made stronger or broken by the stress of life.

Coping with Body Breakdown

In his extraordinarily sensitive book *Who Dies?* Stephen Levine investigates the deep personal meanings of conscious living and conscious dying. Through his therapeutic work with patients who are terminally ill, he provides us with a road map that can guide all our moments of living from now until the end. As one patient who was waiting for a diagnosis said, "Whether I am to die soon or whether I have a long time yet to live, it is clear to me now that I have exactly the same inner work to do." What is this vital work — this attitude that we need to gracefully approach our own illness, disabilities, and ultimate death?

One of the truths we tend to avoid is the reality of death. We tend to run from that reality whenever we can, but we all know we can never really deny it. We all die. We all get ill. Ninety-five percent of us become disabled at some time in our lives. There is such widespread fear related to illness, aging, and death, that people often shun those who are handicapped. In their prejudice, they look down on those who have obvious disabilities, and they prefer to forget that "we are the temporarily able-bodied." To change the negative attitude toward people who are infirm requires a lot of work. In our society, there is a tendency to blame the patient for his or her infirmity. Although it is certainly true that our habits influence our state of health and our emotions influence our physical well-being, in no way should we ever hold a patient responsible for being sick. Much as we would like to have that control, we can never fulfill our illusion: our desire to live happily ever after, to live on to infinity, disease free. As Bernie Siegel points out, meditators die; vegetarians die; athletes die; yogis die. So when your turn comes to confront illness in the family or in yourself, it is important to remember: *No blame!*

In coping with illness and the degeneration of your body, whether that is a slow or a rapid process, your aim is to maintain as much wellness as possible. You may need to let go of the injury to your self-esteem that naturally happens when your body weakens. After all, if you are 25 percent dysfunctional, that is, if you can no longer do a quarter of the things you used to be able to do, that means you are 75 percent functional. So on with it; on with life! When you know where the weak links are in your own organic system, then the most crucial question arises: how do you live most effectively and get the most mileage from your body? With the onset of illness or physical disability, there will be a major transition in your life. You need to recognize this time of transition and honor the changes that life requires of you. It may require some sort of rite of passage.

Psychologically, transitions require letting go of the past and preparing for a new and different future. Grieving for what can no longer be and for your own lost abilities and freedom is one of the things that occurs. When a patient must adjust to life in a wheelchair, for example, she or he has need to mourn the freedom that walking had always been. Loss of mobility and freedom is a time of sadness. Yet eventually you must also let go of the sadness itself. After the sorrowing time, your transition will lead to new readiness to move on. Then the focus becomes how to *learn new ways* to adapt, to find new sources of courage and fulfillment, and to develop new practical methods to do as much as you can. In coping with illness or disability, you will develop a sense of mastery if you try to accomplish as much as possible despite your physical limitations.

In coping with illness or injury, it is beneficial for a patient to turn to her resource people and wonder, "What do the professionals have to say?" These resources include the whole range of medical people: physicians, nurses, rehabilitation staff. Other people who may prove to be helpful include physical education coaches and nutritionists. Since experts sometimes give conflicting advice, the patient will need to sift through the various opinions, trying those that seem reasonable and letting her own body be the guide as to which methods are most effective. Remember, as dancers and athletes do, that you can learn from injuries and pain. The purpose of pain as a sensation is to guide and direct both movement and rest. Of course, rest is a key to recuperation from any bodily harm. In almost every state of health or illness, exercise is also a vital factor. Even minimal exercise has its place. Right up to the point of coma or utter paralysis, some activity can be stimulating and healthful. Maybe all a patient can do is wiggle her toes or raise her eyebrows, but even that amount of exercise can activate her nervous system and stimulate her endocrine glands.

With any program of increased exercise, it is important to begin gradually and not to overdo the initial sessions. (Remember, we usually don't feel the sore muscles from a physical workout until two days later.) In yoga, they give a wise prescription: *stretch yourself just to your limits of comfort, then just a little bit further.* If you practice this approach consistently, you will accomplish your goals through gradual improvement.

Listening to Your Body

Whether we are healthy or ill, our aim should always be to cooperate with the body. The body's aim is to ground us and keep us balanced, so it is important to be honest in this dialog with the physical self. Eugene Gendlin reminds us that we need both to listen and, sometimes, to coax the body. We especially need to listen to the subtle clues the body sends us from its psychosomatic wisdom. For example, when we get a "felt sense" or an "inner stirring," it may be the body's physical (unconscious) reaction to something we have been (consciously) thinking. We need to be open and aware as we ask ourselves about the deep meanings of our symptoms and stirrings. If you are making some plans, for example, ask: Does the body feel "right" when the mind thinks about going ahead? Is there a surge of relief? A feeling of freedom? A small bit of life-energy? A whiff of fresh air? If not, where are the constrictions? What feels stifling? What is blocking the movement toward progress right now?

The body's unconscious messages can sometimes help to determine the optimal treatment program, as Bernie Siegel points out. To listen to your body, you need to be patient and receptive. Can you listen for its metaphors? It may take months or even years to learn the language of your body. For example, a narcoleptic patient dreamed of a small child who threw away his cup of coffee. In exploring the meaning of that dream and how it related to his symptoms, he began to notice and understand that his bouts of daytime sleepiness were triggered when he was suddenly made to feel like a small child, alone and afraid. Several years later, he came to realize that the dream was also suggesting that he would do better if he gave up caffeine. Both insights were helpful for coping with his illness.

The body is very specific in its knowledge of our needs. When we make the effort to cooperate with it, the body can be a faithful ally. It gives of its strength throughout life. We live in union, body, mind, and spirit intimately in relation to each other, and, as we all know, many of the joys of life are body-related. To cope well, we must live life as fully as possible. "LIVE!" says Bernie Siegel. This physician nicely captures the attitude of exceptional (cancer-surviving) patients when he writes about the need to make fun a high priority in life. This fun-loving attitude develops from the essential first step of learning to love yourself. It is never too late for that. Siegel writes that not only does play make you feel good, but it also opens the door to creativity. He urges us: "Choose to love and make others happy, and your life will change, because you will find happiness and love in the process. The first step towards inner peace is to decide to give love."

Healthy Habits for Wellness

While there is great preoccupation with physical fitness in the United States today, where we usually fail is in integration of our wellness programs into our whole way of life. Certainly, most of the population has enough information available to alter their lifestyle in health-promoting ways. What we most frequently need is to look at our lives holistically. We need to recognize the body/mind/spirit as a unity, not as separate; and we need to change the kind of attention we give our bodies. I think either extreme is counterproductive: either to ignore the body, or to go to the other extreme and think obsessively about our bodies and sickness. We need to be aware enough of our habits and their consequences on our health, and we do need to heed the body's warning signals.

Choosing good health habits is an important step in developing and maintaining our bodies for effective coping. We need to look also at the ways we attempt to foster these habits, because attitude makes a difference. Taking on new habits with an attitude of "sacrifice" is not likely to work. Instead we need to view the change as altering old habits and replacing them with habits that will make us more effective, more fully functioning, and therefore more alive. Little by little, we introduce new habits. When we monitor our feelings of well-being, we realize the benefits of this kind of healthy change. Gradually changing to healthy habits is a constant, lifelong process. Developing the capacity to create new habits is fundamental for mastering the art of coping. Coping well, by the most effective use of the body as it changes, is fundamental in the art of living.

6

The Inner Computer
and Its Ways

— ❖ —

I
N THE TAO OF COPING, the stream of the intellect provides a very
important current. There are many ways to think about the intellect, that is, to think about thinking. When we use the metaphor
of the computer to refer to our intellectual processes, we must remember that human intellect, with all its subtle possibilities, is far beyond
what any computer is able to mimic. As the Dalai Lama once said, the
intellect is key to our universal search for happiness and our attempts
to eliminate suffering.

A man sat in my office, quite excited about a dream in which he first
heard a sound, a pure melodious low note that seemed to call him and
show him the way to find Truth. He followed the sound, until he came
to a shady place where he discovered that a large flat slab of stone
beamed the tone that he had followed. He seated himself before the
stone, which was like an altar. Then five lights appeared in a semicircle
on the altar. They seemed to be flames but there were no candles or
lamps visible that could produce the flame. He awoke then with a sense
of vital knowing: "There are five kinds of truth," he said, "(1) factual
truth; (2) inner truth about thoughts, beliefs, opinions; (3) the truth
one tells others based on those thoughts, beliefs and opinions; (4) self-
knowledge about feelings and insights related to one's past and present
experiences; and (5) openness and truth about feelings and experiences
that one shares with others."

As we began to discuss this dream, I realized the wisdom of these
classifications. Thoughts and feelings are indeed quite different. So often our misunderstandings and arguments about "Truth" may be due
to a lack of differentiation between thoughts and feelings. We may also
fail to recognize that others' perceptions vary. Certainly there are *factual realities* that we all agree upon: these are things we can measure.

127

On the other hand, *inner truth* is a much more individual process. It is a fallacy to believe that our own thoughts are "THE Truth." In actuality, each of us formulates beliefs and opinions based on our education and life experience. To be true to ourselves, we need to be inwardly honest, which requires clarity about our own unique view, awareness of the underlying assumptions that we make, and an appreciation of the relativity of that view. Each individual has a right to his or her own inner truth.

The truth you tell others is a subgroup of your thoughts, beliefs, opinions, and attitudes. How much you are willing to divulge depends on your life situation and on your *persona,* that is, the part of your personality that you show to the outside world. Some people have a false persona: what they express to others may differ markedly from what they really think and believe. All people have some kind of image they want to display, but to have a true persona, the thoughts and opinions you express must be congruent, or in tune with the inner truth as you know it. If you are thinking one thing but telling people something entirely different, you are not being true to yourself or to others.

Self-knowledge is the result of exploring and reflecting on your *feelings* and on *patterns of behavior* that you tend to repeat. You can begin by asking, "Am I mad, sad, glad, or afraid?" You will discover numerous subtle variations within those four broad categories. Then you gain by wondering about the inner connections: What triggers these feelings? What influences these moods? Most often your emotional life is dramatically related to your thoughts and your interactions with other people. When you search for insight about your relationships and the behavioral patterns in which you get caught, you are using your analytic mind to increase your sensitivity and broaden the scope of your options. In this way self-knowledge leads to freedom. Finally, *openness and truth about feelings* is the most challenging and productive form of truth because it provides a means to interpersonal intimacy and trust. All told, to be free to share yourself with others, it is vital to be a reflective person. Then you understand yourself and your relationship to your environment. You begin to see your life in perspective and can share your truths with others.

As the dream suggested, there is deep wisdom in the psyche, and inner Truth is at the core of coping well. Just as there is no "ONE Truth," so also there is no "one way" to cope. When you reflect on the process of coping, you accomplish three things. First, you learn to know yourself much better and to appreciate your strengths at the same time that you recognize your limitations. Second, you cope more effectively because you can identify which of those limitations may be self-imposed. And, third, you can choose more wisely from the array of coping methods those that are most likely to be useful for you in your present situation.

Problem Analysis

In vibrant, effective coping, the intellect is the control mechanism of the entire process. We use the intellect first to identify the problem, next to consider the possible alternatives for solution, then to devise plans and implement them, and finally to evaluate progress and to plan future steps. In many ways, the first step may be the most crucial. When we can think clearly and specify the nature of the problem, the pieces of the solution often fall into place much more easily.

The basic question under consideration is: *What is the problem?* The following questions and comments can be useful guides in analysis of your own current and future problems. The aim is to analyze the situation, to focus and to identify the sources of difficulty. So consider the following:

• *Is it a task difficulty?* Tasks differ in what they require. Most tasks require thought and effort. Does your task require more effort? Or perhaps what you need is to withdraw your overly effortful striving? Do you need more information? Is a solo approach likely to be most successful? Or do you need to cooperate with others? What other things might this task ask? Or is it, perhaps, task overload? If so, how can you prioritize? Delegate? Minimize the nonessentials? What resources are available for help?

• *It it a decisional problem?* Do you have some important decision to make? What values are involved? Have you listed and weighed all the alternatives? Is a creative solution or compromise possible? And how do *you* usually come to a decision? Have you "slept on it"? Or are you possibly obsessed or ruminating about it? (Note: people with strong thinking abilities often have difficulty coming to decisions and making commitments.)

• *Is it a transitional problem?* Does your current situation require a change in lifestyle? What changes do you need to make so that you can live life in the present and life in the future gracefully? (Note: depression is usually a result of some resistance to change. We can think of many of the losses that occur later in life alternatively as transition points into yet another stage of life.) Navigation through the transition requires acceptance of the realities. When you decide to view change positively, you can more easily search for creative ways to adapt.

• *Is it a personal unmet need?* Have you become stuck in some feeling state that is unpleasant? Are you feeling bored and uninvolved? Or perhaps you have been overstimulated? Have you felt put down (by others) or inadequate (putting yourself down)? Is there a growth need that you have not yet recognized? What else might you need just for you, for example, rest, learning, increased, or decreased involvement, support, or "letting go"?

• *Is the problem relational?* Is this an interpersonal difficulty? How important is this other person in your life? Does the relationship require intervention? Does the other person need more of your time and attention? Or would it be better if you back off? Is more communication needed? Or better quality of communication? Less criticism? More assertiveness? Or more acceptance? (Note: if something you're doing consistently isn't working, then it will most likely be better if you *do something different!*)

• *Is this a systemic problem?* Is more than a single relationship involved? Are three people involved in repetitive triangles, that is, do you recognize patterns of conflictual behavior? More than three people? Is it a problem in the family system? In the extended family? Or in the work system? In the wider social system? How much control do you realistically have? (Remember: you can change no one but yourself!) What do you need to know in order to choose the best strategy for coping with the system you are in?

• *Is this a medical problem?* What is involved in getting yourself (or another person) to appropriate treatment? Is a second medical opinion needed? How do you communicate with the professional caregivers? Do you trust the physicians and have faith in your recovery? Are you using all available health measures? Are you committed to doing whatever is necessary to facilitate recovery? (Note: it is important to *balance* assertiveness and expression of your own perceptions with trust and appropriate dependence. In hospitals, you are generally expected to be docile. Caregivers want you to allow them to care for you in the ways they know best. You must bring an attitude of cooperation, but also you need to communicate body awareness, past history, and current complicating factors. Hospital staff sometimes forget that the patient's psychological need for internal control and self-mastery lasts right up until death.) Keep in mind that you are responsible for communicating your own needs, but the hospital staff feels responsible for your medical care. Ultimately, this is the crucial negotiation.

• *Is there a spiritual need?* Does your situation provoke guilt or a moral dilemma? Is there a hunger for spiritual growth and development? Do you need to reassess your personal commitments in the light of your sense of the purpose of life? Is it time to rethink your theology? What do you really believe? What *is* the meaning of your life? What is your primary purpose at this stage of your life?

These focus questions are part of a thought process that aims to make a thorough appraisal of the situation by asking not only, "Am I in trouble?" or "Could I be in trouble in the future?" but also "What can be done about the situation to improve my chances for functioning most effectively and to increase the state of well-being for all concerned?"

After assessing the situation to determine the nature of the problem, the "What can be done?" ideas rapidly follow. Usually many possibilities exist, but not all of them are practical or achievable. Researchers Lazarus and Folkman define this stage of appraisal as: "a complex evaluative process that takes into account which coping options are available, the likelihood that a given coping option will accomplish what it is supposed to, and the likelihood that one can apply a particular strategy or set of strategies effectively." So, when you assess the coping options, you need to take into account the probability of success: "Is the strategy I am thinking of likely to be effective?" And, equally important, "Can I pull it off?"

When you ask yourself, *"Can I do what I am attempting to do?"* you are asking a key question that social psychologists call "efficacy expectation." How you answer that question depends on your level of self-esteem and on your mood or emotion at the moment. In those times when you are feeling depressed or anxious, your estimation of your capacity to function effectively may be diminished. But having doubts is not sufficient reason to rule out an option. Many times a "long shot" is worth attempting. Many times, too, you will find that confidence comes as a result of attempting something and seeing gradual progress in a new and positive direction.

Consider the following example: Jackie, a patient with lupus, initially had a very difficult time learning to adjust. She was the mother of two small children, and it was very hard for her to tell family and friends about her disease. Talking about lupus made her feel very sorrowful and anxious. She had to learn both to live with the disease and with her fear that it would worsen. In order to cope, she had begun reading and going to lectures about lupus progression and exacerbation. Her two greatest fears were that she would not be able to raise her children independently and that she would become so incapacitated that she would be dependent on others.

For several years Jackie was incapacitated much of the time. The doctor told her to rest and to do as little as possible. Almost any exertion led to severe chest pain and breathing difficulties. It was as though her worst fears were being realized. Her anxiety tended to make her even more tight in the chest, and there was a spiral effect between disease symptoms and the physiological aspects of her anxiety.

Over a period of time, Jackie's determination to master her disease grew strong. She thought hard about what she could do and gradually began to push herself gently beyond her limits of comfort. She realized she could do more than she had estimated and was determined to return to fully functioning motherhood. She did not want her children to wonder why their mom could not be at school when they were in a concert or play. Nor did she want them to have to forego dancing class or swimming lessons for lack of chauffeuring. She found that she could, in fact, cope with more activity. Her pace of increase was gradual, and she was careful not to overdo.

When the children were both in high school, Jackie reassessed her capabilities and took on a part-time job to put some money toward college tuitions. By the time the second child was off to college, Jackie was ready for full-time work. She took a job in hospital administration, beginning a career in social service, which she enjoyed. Looking back at the effect that lupus had had in her life, Jackie realized that the early stages were the worst. Now she was fully functioning almost all of the time. Her life was full and rich, and only occasionally did she have to stop and rest. "I'm doing almost as much as any other fifty-year-old," she said. "I never could have believed it possible when this all started twenty years ago."

Not every chronic disease patient will be so fortunate as to master most of its challenges. Even the fortunate ones will always need to be very careful about their health, but the important point is that the way we think about the challenges markedly affects our capacity to cope and the ways we choose to go about those tasks. A person like Jackie, who has good capacity to think through problems as well as determination to master the challenges, is halfway there when it comes to finding or developing solutions.

Woody Guthrie was such a man. Woody and his son, Arlo, both fabulously popular musicians, were both eventually laid low by the unconquerable effects of Huntington's Chorea. This neurological disease starts with muscle weakness that makes the person stagger in a way that is often mistaken for drunkenness. It ends with dementia severe enough to require permanent hospitalization, usually on a psychiatric ward for the mentally incompetent. Yet Woody lived courageously and fully. His music is flavored with the attitude that helped him cope as long as he was able. He wrote songs about courage and self-esteem. He hated the idea that "you're a born loser." Rather he saw that, when life hits you hard, you need to resound with songs that give you pride and belief that "this is your world." Such are the songs that we all need to sing as we find our way, sometimes stumbling or slipping, but courageously returning to resume our direction along life's path. The way we think about our problems, the inner songs we sing, and the words we use have impact on how much courage we can muster.

Woody Guthrie and the mother with lupus are examples of people who have sufficient "ego strength" to cope well with very difficult situations. As Harvard scholar Robert W. White tells us, a person with ego strength is one who is able to use his or her mental capacities without undue emotional interference. (The "ego" is a concept that we can think about as the "inner executive" or "the mastermind computer" within the personality. The ego is both the observer and the decision-maker within each of us.) So ego strength does *not* mean being puffed up or self-important. Rather, it means having good contact with reality, clear perceptions, and good judgment. People with ego strength have good relationships with others and well-functioning internal defenses that prevent overstimulation and that "overwhelmed" feeling. Such people are able to think clearly, to learn well, and to avoid impulsive behavior that would be immature or childish. Ego strength means having a sense of self-control and mastery over one's own thoughts and feelings. All told, ego strength is defined as "the power to rally from setback and generally cope with adversity."

When your ego is strong, you are able to integrate and compare

information from many sources. You are good at coping, able to observe your own thoughts, feelings, and behavior and able to make the
adjustments you need as you go along. A strong ego means you can
obtain the information you must have in your decision-making process.
You can easily interface with the external world by asking first, "What
information do I need?" and "What resource people do I need?"

When interfacing with the environment, you need to consider the
very important issue of your time frame for getting help. This involves
determining when the resources you need may be available. It also involves considering your own deadlines in getting assistance. The often
excessive busyness of others can have an impact on your time strategy, so you may have to adjust your requests for assistance based on
the availability of your helpers. You will undoubtedly have to operate
with some degree of flexibility. If you make a rigid attempt to maintain
control of circumstances, you are doomed from the start to frustration
and failure.

In making the many decisions required for effective coping, there are
frequently times when you must weigh *priorities*. In order to prioritize
your actions, it is a good idea to ask several times each day:

- What must be done right away? Or very soon?

- What will my current emotional and physical state allow me to
  tackle now?

- What can I postpone until I am stronger? Until I have more time?
  Until I have additional information?

- In what ways can I wait and watch to see what unfolds?

These questions are closely associated with determining what actions you need to take and in what order. Other factors to consider in
making decisions about action relate to the broader perspective of your
life. To plan with a long-range perspective in mind, you need to reflect
on your overall purposes. You ask:

- What general strategy should I follow?

- What are my long-term goals or aims?

- What are my short-term objectives?

- What are the first, second, and third steps I should take?

- What contingency plans do I need?

- What is my usual work style and time frame? Is that likely to be effective in this situation?

Like a chess player, you need to plan your moves ahead. That means guessing about the "yet unknown" and making some judgments about probabilities. Since the pace of living is often terribly rapid when you are coping with particularly difficult times, it is a good idea to take time out whenever possible to assess where you are and where you are going. *Contingency plans* allow you to make flexible yet rapid responses to life's unpredictable circumstances. The key is to look at the possible and probable happenings and then to decide in advance, "If this..., then I'll do that...." When you know ahead of time which course you will take under several of the most likely circumstances, you will be much more able to face the future without excessive fear.

The final step in masterminding the coping process is to *assess how things are going*. In actuality, this type of assessment should occur at fairly frequent intervals, perhaps optimally on a daily basis. Evaluation involves listening to feedback from the environment and reflecting:

- How do others respond to what I do?

- Can I move ahead?

- Should I alter direction to accommodate resistance?

- What other routes take me to where I want to go?

- Do I need to retreat?

- How effectively am I responding to the current demands?

This evaluative type of thinking becomes part of a feedback loop, linking to your plan of action as an ongoing process. It seems that a certain amount of this evaluative process is what occurs during your nighttime dreaming. When you to sleep on a decision or when you need extra sleep during times of heavy stress, it is likely that your unconscious mind is adding its holistic perspective to your conscious thought-out evaluation.

Finally, this analysis and self-evaluation need to include the important aspect of recognizing and *rewarding yourself* for coping effectively. This is vital! To keep going when the going is rough, you will need to feel the effects of consistent positive reinforcements. Other people may forget to tell you, so you may need to be your own best booster. This self-affirmation does not mean inaccurate, narcissistic self-aggrandizement. Rather it means telling yourself as you go along, "I can cope. I *am* coping!" These affirmations are very effective in providing the strength and courage to continue the push when life's moments are toughest.

As you reflect during your self-evaluation, you will need the honesty to see your imperfections without loss of self-esteem. Can you allow yourself to see the humor in your "bloopers" and your faux pas? None of us is perfect. Don't forget how vitally important it is to recognize your essential okayness and worth. Your human worth and beauty lies, not in any illusory perfection, but in the very fact of trying to do your best and holding onto hope, especially when that's not easy.

In his practical and inspiring book *Winning Life's Toughest Battles*, psychologist Julius Segal makes a similar point. Segal has done extensive studies with ordinary people who have survived extraordinary stress, such as hostages and prisoners of war. From this research came the understanding that hope and survival go together. We must shed self-blame and hold on to the hope in our hearts. Segal suggests that tenacious optimism may increase survival potential by actually changing body chemistry.

The way in which you think about your capacity to cope is all important. So the life-giving affirmations to program into the brain as part of the coping evaluation are:

- I'm okay.

- I can cope.

- I *am* coping!

- I'm going to continue to be okay.

As psychiatrist Jerome Frank has discovered, faith is the most important component of healing. Whether that is faith in a cause, in a divinity, or in a healer seems to matter less than the very presence of faith itself. In similar fashion, we can now say that faith, and in particular faith in oneself and in one's capacity to cope, is probably the most significant component of coping effectively. "I *can* cope. I *am* coping." These are the affirmations of strength and trust that are so vital.

The Coping Model as Cognitive Map

When you feel lost and need directions, you are like one who has no map. Emotionally, when you are facing life's toughest challenges, you may be like a confused traveler. You may know the present position you are in: often anxious, disappointed, full of frustration, grief, and/or anguish. What you need is a map to help you to get to where you yearn to be: serene, with a sense of inner harmony, at peace with your world. The coping model presented in this book is one way of thinking about how to get from where you are to where you want to be. It is a cognitive map, or way of organizing your thinking, a way of linking your thoughts about the problem to those coping resources that can be most beneficial. It can be helpful to ask yourself the following questions to orient yourself in the direction in which you need to move.

• Is part of the problem an *overload of emotion* right now? If so, in what way can I use the arts to help me regain emotional composure so that I can get back to the tasks and challenges of living?

Internally, in what way can I use humor, or imagery, or creativity, or participation in any of the arts to help calm myself and achieve a steady state of emotional balance? (See chapter 2)

And externally, to whom can I reach out for support and nurturance? Who brings joy, comfort, and love into my life? What members of my family or friendship network can I contact? And what is the best way to contact them? Is there a support group that would hear me and help me meet my needs? Is there someone who will listen to my anxieties, frustrations, and sorrows until these feelings dissipate and I return to a more cheerful countenance? (See chapter 3)

• Am I feeling *out of balance*? Would my situation be improved if I were to seek balance and harmony within myself and with the wider world?

Spiritually, in what ways could meditation, prayer, or contemplation be of use to me right now? How might my attitudes and feelings change if I were to look upward, seeking the guidance of God or of a Higher Power?

Would my philosophy of life and my sense of purpose or meaning shift if I were to look deeply inward, seeking integrity and inspiration? (See chapter 4)

And *physically*, is my body too tense or feeling out of sorts? Would a change of diet, exercise, or sleep patterns be beneficial and manageable? When can I find time to relax? And what relaxation exercises would be best for me to incorporate into my daily routine? What brief method of relaxation can I use when I need comfort? What can I do to relax right now? (See chapter 5)

•Certainly this *problem situation* requires clear thinking. Internally I will continue to organize my thoughts to identify the many aspects of the situation and to find specific strategies to ameliorate the difficulties. How can I break the overall problem into smaller, more manageable pieces? As I go along, how can I reward myself for coping well?

And externally, I need to be increasingly aware of resources in the environment that can provide help. Where can I find information I need? Who are the people who will provide necessary services? (See chapter 7)

When you run through such an inventory of questions to yourself, you are able to clarify not only the nature of the problem, but also a whole array of coping strategies and resources that you can pull forth as needed. Within any one category, there is a wide range of methods to use.

Choice and Variety in Coping Styles

Yours is the choice. You are the individual who must contend with your own particular combination of circumstances. No one else can tell you what you should do (though many friends and family members may try to assume the responsibility of choice for you). The most sensible way to accept advice from others is to view it as creative input. Research shows that not only are there a variety of coping styles, but also that different groups of people gravitate toward different coping methods. As you think about coping and evaluate your own style in relation to others, you need to be aware that certain aspects of your coping style are related to your cultural background and to the sub-cultural groups to which you belong. The importance of cultural context arises because most coping responses are learned behaviors. On the other hand, some aspects of your choice of coping methods are related to your basic personality style.

In any one family, there are often several different ways of coping with similar circumstances. Many people fall into a trap by assuming that another person is coping poorly just because his or her way of managing events is different from their own. Much family conflict could be avoided by the simple realization that people differ and that each has a choice in making a uniquely personal response to the life stressors that are present.

One family that I know is noted for being especially effective in coping with difficulties. Each member of the family has undergone numerous trials, but they seem to come up time and again, bubbling with energy, courage, and good humor. One family member sees life as "a challenge to be lived," rather than as "a problem to be solved." In fact, he tells me good-naturedly that he isn't sure he likes the word "coping" because, for him, that implies a "problem." This man tends to minimize problems; he does not deny their existence, however. He told me that his father had died when he was ten, leaving his mother to bring up eight children. It is evident that the children have all grown up influenced by their mother's positive attitude and extraordinary capacities for coping. One sister is task-oriented in her coping style, so she quickly sets about making necessary arrangements. Others in the family make it their priority to discuss their feelings or their philosophies about the meaning of life and death. When someone dies, for example, they wonder together: how can they integrate what has happened in their family with their religious views of a loving God? For all of them it is important to spend time talking together. They reach inside, at a deep and personal level, to grapple with the cosmic issues and to dialog, providing both meaning and emotional support for one another.

Thinking about Personality

There are often similarities as well as differences in coping among individuals within any one family. Both the similarities and differences in coping style are necessary and appropriate. Personality, which comes both from genetic inheritance and from experiences in early life, contributes to these individual styles. The way we think and the intensity of our feelings flow from our distinct personalities. Some of us are more oriented toward thinking things through, whereas others are more emotional, both in how we perceive things and in how we come to make our decisions. Of course, every one of us has the capacity both to think and to feel; but, when we're in a thinking mode, we may be unaware of feelings; and conversely, when we are in a powerful feeling state, thinking tends to be out of consciousness.

The strength of a predominantly *thinking type* of person is the clarity and precision in his or her organization and presentation of ideas. The life of such a person is mainly governed by reflection. Thinking types generally are excellent at establishing structured order. They make judgments based on facts and they bring clarity to a situation that tends to reduce the likelihood of emotional overload. On the negative side, a person with a strong thinking style may be obsessional, rigid, and overzealous, or pedantic and dull. He or she may be a strict adherent to a system of rules and may attempt to coerce others with messages of "ought," "should," and "must." Since thinking types tend to be most tyrannical in their control over themselves, they often have difficulties in making decisions and commitments to a single course of action. On the other hand, the primary asset of the thinking person is the ability to *analyze* and break a problem into bite-size pieces. When a problem is thereby "chunked down" into its component parts, it often becomes much more manageable.

In contrast, the tendency of the *feeling type* is to view situations from a global, emotional point of view. The feeling type person's way of using the mind is diffuse, *impressionistic,* and lacking in sharp detail. Rather than the active, intense, and sharply focused attention of the thinker, the feeling type person tends to respond quickly to what is immediately impressive, striking, or obvious.

For fully effective coping, it is vital to have and to use both thinking and feeling functions harmoniously. Just as it is useful for thinking types to develop their emotional life by communicating feelings to the people around them, so also it is important for feeling types to develop their intellectual coping potentials. In fact, the use of the intellect is one important way that overwhelming feelings can be controlled. I often tell people who are feeling types that when they find themselves swarming with emotion and feeling inundated, then is the time to tell themselves: "Stop and think!" When you break the problem down into little chunks, the emotion almost invariably evaporates or becomes much more manageable.

Reframing and Restructuring

When we look at our lives from a broad perspective, we often see that there are changes that we may want and need to make. For example, most of us have grown up with the habit of thinking far too negatively.

This is undoubtedly the result of all the "shoulds" and "oughts" and "musts" we internalized from presumably well-meaning teachers and parents who were trying to mold us into behaving in socially acceptable ways. While critiques surely had a purpose during our growing-up years, most negativities are far too heavy and oppressive to carry around in adulthood. Too many people ask themselves habitually, "Where have I gone wrong?" When you carry the baggage of negative thought patterns, this burden adds significantly to any tendency you might have to feel chronically anxious, angry, and/or depressed. The simple, sensible answer is to let go of the burden. Realistically, changing the burdensome way you think may not be a quick or easy change, however. One man, who constantly berated himself and felt worthless, had a dream in which he saw himself imprisoned within the body of a powerful Nazi soldier. That was a clear image of how stuck he felt within the pattern of oppressive self-derogation.

Thought habits may be quite pervasive, and the first step is to become aware of the way you are thinking. One experiment you might try is to spend a whole week with the following assignment: *Avoid thinking any thoughts that are critical, complaining, or defensive.* You will be amazed to discover just how you spend your free thinking time. When such negative thoughts come into awareness, simply note their occurrence and make the choice to stop and think about something else.

Therapists who work with people who are trying to change their lives, know that thought, emotion, and behavior are all linked. This means that when you change the way you think, changes in feeling and behavior follow naturally. Similarly, when you change your behavior, it will have an effect on both your thoughts and your emotions. (All three are governed by an interrelated system within the brain, so that a change in any part of the system will effect changes in the other aspects that are connected.) Therefore, one way of making major life changes is by altering your viewpoint about problems. This is what we call *reframing*, that is, a way of reorganizing your understanding of a situation such that you are able to reinterpret the meaning of events. When a person reframes his or her thoughts, the meaning of life experience is altered in such a way that more positive potentials and behavior change can come to the fore.

Consider the example of a certain highly successful salesman. He tends to reframe most events in a *hopeful* and *helpful* manner. When I asked about how he copes with customer sales resistance, he was thoughtful but then responded quickly: "I understand that people have a natural fear of the slick, money-making salesman. I never view my work that way. In fact, my attitude toward any sales promotion is primarily based on the *service* that I offer to the customer."

I could sense his sincerity and was not surprised when he added, "This is not just a sales gimmick. The customer would know. Most people can see right through a phony attitude. Rather, it's a real attitude, a real orientation toward service for the customer." He told me that his company makes presentations at conventions for educational products. He said, "We tell them about our competitor's products too. We try to evaluate them all honestly. If we don't have a better product than our competitors do, then we don't deserve to be in the business."

With such an attitude, the naturally competitive situation of sales meetings becomes instead an avenue to express helpfulness and genuine hope. This form of reframing can be a highly significant contribution to one's sense of personal integrity and successful salesmanship as well.

In reframing thoughts, we look at life from the positive perspective. Here is another example: A large percentage of the adult American population is single at any one time. Some find themselves plagued by feelings of loneliness. Others view their lives as full of precious freedom — freedom either to enjoy solitude or to engage in activities that they themselves choose. You can think of being alone as loneliness and suffering, or you can reframe it as joyful opportunity.

A great deal of coping strength depends on the way you look at things. Your attitude and habits significantly relate to your outlook on life. Be honest with yourself and ask: When something comes up, do I call it "a difficulty," "a problem," "a frustration," or "a challenge"? Research shows that those who view a situation as a *challenge* cope better than those who generally use more negative descriptions. Lazarus and Folkman write that when you view a stress as a challenge, this appraisal allows you to mobilize your best coping efforts. What you call a challenge focuses on your potential for inherent gain or growth. The result is pleasurable emotions such as eagerness, excitement, and exhilaration. Your eagerness to master a situation is in sharp contrast to situations that you might view as "a threat" or some form of "harm or loss." In the latter case, you are more likely to feel the negative emotions, including anxiety and grief. Chronic negative thought patterns lead to depression and hopelessness. When you reframe your thoughts to focus on growth opportunities and potential for mastery, new liveliness and new energies emerge.

Mastery and the Internal Locus of Control

Lazarus and Folkman write: "The joy of challenge is that one pits oneself against the odds." They show also that the capacity to think of our difficulties as "challenges that can be mastered" is closely related to the efforts we put forth and to our sense of control in our lives. Psychologist J. B. Rotter called this characteristic way of viewing situations the "internal locus of control."

When you encounter adversity, there may be little realistic opportunity to alter the course of events. In this case, you may feel helpless and powerless. One way to reframe that situation is to define the challenge as one of *controlling oneself* in the face of adversity and even of transcending it. With debilitating illness, for example, or the death of a loved one, the person who copes well may make it a challenge to maintain a positive outlook, or to tolerate pain and distress without excessive complaining.

Eleanor was a person who could take up a challenge. She had come to the United States from a middle European country when she was seventeen, beginning her work here as an *au pair*. Gradually she worked her way into nursing and obtained all the training she could get. After her college diploma, she went on for a master's degree and eventually a doctorate in nursing. By midlife, she was teaching in a foremost nursing school.

I met Eleanor when she was seventy-eight years old. She was then, and had always been, a single professional woman. She had also been coping with cancer herself for over thirty years. She had just had her second mastectomy. She attended a group workshop in which cancer patients were learning about nutrition, exercise, and the healing use of imagery. Eleanor came to the group with a cane. She seemed somewhat dejected and walked in a bent-over manner. What frightened Eleanor about cancer, even more than the pain, the medical complications, and the insurance hassles, was the thought of dying alone. She hadn't minded being single, but it terrified her to think of being alone while she was dying.

As she told her life story, Eleanor mentioned the many young nurses for whom she had acted as mentor over the years. One member of the group reflected, "Eleanor, you're not alone. You have a whole network of people who are there helping you. You're a real people person! Why, every time you describe one of the complications you've had with your illness, you talk about information or help you received from one or another of your former students." Eleanor brightened up. She knew this assessment of her was correct. She was indeed connected with hundreds of people who could be resources and provide support for her.

Later that evening, Eleanor showed her true spirit. The staff had planned a musical event. As all the patients gathered to hear the music, Eleanor took up the self-initiated challenge. She began to dance. Cane and all, she danced her way into the circle. Then she drew others in. She took them by the hands and they too began dancing. One by one, patients and staff alike were drawn in by Eleanor's magnetism. If Eleanor could dance like that, twirling her cane when she did not actually need it for support, then every member of the group could take up a similar challenge. Courage and a challenge to create a sense of community had moved this elderly woman. She was no longer feeling alone. All were inspired and all joined her in the enjoyment of the moment. Now, as always, her challenge was clear: to live as fully as possible and, despite limitations, make all she could of herself. We silently cheered her on as we joined her in the dance.

Julius Segal also writes about the inherent power that is available when one seizes the initiative. In studying hostages, prisoners of war, and others who struggle with life's toughest battles, Segal came to recognize the importance of a sense of personal control. He writes:

> Try to imagine yourself as a captive. The activities you take for granted are no longer under your control. You cannot eat when you are hungry, enjoy a walk or a nap when you feel like it, or even urinate or defecate when nature calls. Your entire life has slipped out of your grasp.
>
> Most of the POWs...say that the realization they had lost command over their existence was the really awful thing about their ordeal. Losing control over their daily lives was more critical than their more exotic and publicized sufferings — the threats of execution, hunger, beatings, torture and isolation....
>
> Those captives who triumphed over their adversity have a lesson to teach us all: They managed somehow to reassert a degree of command over their destiny. Instead of becoming totally pas-

sive and helpless, they fastened on every opportunity they could find to reaffirm their lost power.

Eleanor, like the captives that Segal interviewed, found a small way to assert herself, gaining a sense of her personal power by seizing the initiative. That is true for all of us. No matter what your circumstances, there is always some small thing you can do by your own choice. There is always at least some small way in which you can act from an individual sense of internal locus of control.

There is a great deal of research evidence that people who are caught in a sense of their own helplessness fall easily into a depressive state. They have lost the sense of their own internal locus of control. As Rotter suggested, they may tend to view events as under the control of powerful others or as due to chance or fate. People who have an expectation that all control resides in external forces tend to view life as unpredictable and vastly complex. They lack self-confidence and may suffer from inferiority feelings. Psychologists have found there is a significant correlation between depressive tendencies, on the one hand, and the tendency to view all the rewards in life as in the control of others.

Although the experience of loss of control and helplessness may be natural and common in certain stressful situations, you do not have to remain forever caught in those powerless feelings. When you have medical illness or have experienced some major loss, these stressors tend, at least initially, to make you feel that you have lost control over your life. However, we know that you will cope most successfully when you can work on your thought patterns in order to regain an internal locus of control, reestablishing a sense of mastery in your life.

People who have a sense of internal locus of control can rather quickly regain a feeling of personal mastery. They are often able to recognize the relationship between their own behavior and the rewards that they can obtain in life. Even in small ways, when you realize that your own actions can lead to positive results, you will find that confidence and a sense of power naturally arise. Robert W. White calls this the sense of "effectance." You may remember that feeling in the common experience he describes. Have you ever seen a baby grasping for or crawling after something? In a child's playful, exploratory behavior the child often has a feeling of "the joy in being a cause." For the child, as for the adult who is coping with a new challenge, competence is gradually developed with each successive act of mastery of the environment. Confidence is gained with the recognition of having manipulated and mastered some challenge that presented itself. Successful people in all walks of life and people coping with all sorts of stressors tend to build on their internal sense of being in control, that is, they build on confidence and competence.

This internal locus of control and sense of mastery is terribly important. When you are overwhelmed with tasks and challenges that seem too big, it is essential that you *do not give in to powerlessness*. Rather, do as the scientists do and chunk the problem down to size. Take one small piece of it, address it, conquer it, and experience *mastery*. This gives you the confidence to go on to the next piece. Choose those small areas where *you have control*. In those small areas, recognize your competence. This builds confidence, and soon you will see that your sense of mastery emerges.

The Marvelous Intellect

Scientists and mathematicians know that there is elegance and beauty where the orderly, underlying principles of nature are found amid awesome complexity. Those who study the human body, or especially the human brain, are privileged to witness in depth the workings of an amazing organism. In recent years, the discoveries of neuroscience have greatly expanded our understanding of the brain, which is a powerful, complex, and wonderful instrument. People often think of intellect in much too simplistic terms. For example, most people tend to think of someone with a "high IQ" as "intelligent" and one with a "low IQ" as "stupid." With this outlook it is much too easy to think, "I can't do that; I'm not smart enough." In reality, intellect is far more multifaceted than most of us realize. A single IQ score can hardly do justice to the potential that we all have for intellectual functioning. We are each multi-potentialed and multi-talented. We each have many different aspects of our minds that have been actualized through our training and mental discipline. These areas of the brain are highly developed. On the other hand, we all have areas of the brain that are relatively undeveloped, like fields left fallow. Clearly our brains do differ one from another. Our brains are probably as unique and different as our faces are. Add to that the educational differences that we have encountered while growing up, and you will have some appreciation of the range of human differences. Despite our differences, however, we all share certain capabilities, even in common with the world's greatest geniuses. For example, unless we have suffered some severe brain damage, we all have the capacity to be creative; and we all can and do use our minds in the same way that scientific researchers do.

As we engage in this process of thinking about thinking, we can see that nature's way is wonderful and intricate. The resources of our brains are indeed astounding. Consider the *creative* ways we approach some of the daily hassles we encounter. Think of how readily we can "brainstorm" and conceive of multitudes of ideas, multitudes of ways to handle things. If you are blocked by a traffic accident on your way to work or to the grocery store, for example, how many other routes can you think of that would get you to where you want to go? How many ways can you think of coping with the frustration and tension that situation might bring?

We are indeed creative thinkers. We are also natural *scientists*. If a problem presents itself, for example, the need to obtain a new job, most of us can and do go about it in an orderly fashion. We research the problem by obtaining information from newspapers, head hunters, and friends. We proceed in a step-by-step fashion until we find a solution, that is, until we have found a good match between the needs of the external world for our services and our own needs for income and for work that is fitting. In the process of coping with such ordinary challenges, we use our scientific minds by developing theories (for example, "how I would fit in the marketing world") and doing experiments (for example, going for an interview or taking an internship as a way of "trying on a job for size"). Some experiments fail and we find the job match is no good. Some succeed and we find ourselves on the way to a substantial new career. As scientists, we try to maintain an objective view. No matter how much we may want things to turn out a certain way, each of us as scientist must look at the situation objectively and analyze the results of our actions.

On the whole, we can see that in coping with challenges, we have to draw upon all of our intellectual resources. Our brains are constantly active and ever so intricate in their marvelous workings. We use the forebrain for planning and initiative and the left cortex for analysis of the problem. To imagine possible courses of action, we use the right hemisphere and often the occipital lobe at the back of the head for visualizing options. Both left and right cerebral hemispheres are in constant interaction as we make choices of coping strategies. As we think about our lives, our memories, values, and emotions are all interacting constantly. These components of our mental processes are stored and activated from deep within the brain. All these components constitute the stuff from which are formed our coping abilities and attitudes.

A positive attitude toward coping with the challenges of one's life is a key to opening the doors to all other inner and outer resources. Whatever stage of problem-solving you are in, it is important to remember that your attitude undergirds all other mental activity. When you reframe your thoughts in a positive manner, problems are much easier to solve and your emotions are more easily manageable.

You realize, therefore, when you look at that metaphoric glass of liquid before you, it is life-enhancing to view it as "half full" rather than "half empty." This outlook does not mean a denial of problems or a simple glossing over of difficulties. Rather, your attitude must be based on the truth within yourself. The truth is always multifaceted. Look for the strengths; they will help you to cope. Focus on the competence; this will build confidence that will help you to find ways around the limitations and frustrations. Remember, when one road is blocked, there are usually numerous other roads that you can take.

As aging progresses and death nears, we know that sometimes a person's intellectual capacities may diminish. At that stage of life, the aging person needs others to help do the thinking. Others are needed to clarify situations and help to think problems through to solution. The aging person will naturally want to contribute his or her own thoughts, and these ideas should always be heard and validated by the caretaking others. Those who provide care usually have the responsibility of making decisions. It is important that caretakers remember that the attitudes they bring, as they cope with the aging and mentally incompetent person, have a strong influence on the thinking, feelings, and general well-being of the aged person.

If yours is the task of assisting a person who nears death, remember the importance of reframing. How you think about the process of living and dying continues to be vitally important. For the aging or dying person, the present situation is yet another new phase of life. One's own truth continues to be important until the very last moment of life. How each one thinks about this last challenge of life has much impact on one's final sense of personal integrity.

7

Action Research: The Way of the Warrior

I N OUR CULTURE, the way of the warrior is to follow a modern
hero's journey into the realm of coping. We think of the archetypal hero as a lonesome venturer who goes out to slay the dragon
and rescue the princess. Today's hero more often contends with com-
puters, answering machines, or bureaucracies rather than with dragons,
and the journey is seldom taken totally alone. It is the traditional attitude and courage of the hero that we need in order to become a warrior
and to cope effectively. As Carol Pearson writes in her book *The Hero
Within*, the archetypal warrior is a characteristic within each of us that
is imbued with heroism:

> [When] people have the courage to fight for themselves they
> can affect their worlds.... [It] is possible not only to identify the
> dragon but to slay it: We can take charge of our lives, elimi-
> nate our problems, and make a better world.... This archetype
> helps teach us to claim our power and to assert our identity in
> the world.... Intellectually, the Warrior helps us to speak out and
> to fight for what nourishes our minds, our hearts and our souls,
> and to vanquish those things that sap and deplete the human
> spirit.... The development of warrioring capabilities is essential
> to a full life.

Joseph Campbell also gives us clues to the vital attitudes we need
when he describes the hero's willingness to confront change. He writes
in *The Hero of a Thousand Faces* that "the hero-deed is a continuous
shattering of the crystallization of the moment." The growing point
of the hero requires transformation and "fluidity, not stubborn pon-
derosity." To be a warrior, with the hero's outlook on life, we must be
willing to be active. Rather than surrender to stagnation and feelings
of powerlessness, we must take life by the tail and grapple with it.

Consider Paul, a corporate middle manager who was unexpectedly confronted with the problem of early retirement. His company was cutting back their work force and enticing older employees to retire, by offering a two-year salary bonus. Paul, at age fifty-five, was not ready to retire but the pressure from the company included strong innuendos that those who did not accept the package would be transferred to undesirable locations, given heavy workloads, and stymied in any attempts at career growth or autonomy.

Paul had been with the company for twenty-five years. A great deal of his self-esteem was connected with his work. He considered himself a team player and had been well-respected for the hard work he had always performed. He was a long-range planner by nature as well as training. So he was taken aback by the sudden change in his career status that left him without a plan. He knew he had to accept the early retirement package, but beyond that he had no idea how he would reorder his life. The dragon Paul faced was unemployment. It seemingly lashed out at him with its mythical barbed tail, attacking his self-esteem and sense of well-being.

In a state of high anxiety, Paul approached the corporation career outplacement counselor, who proved to be a valuable initial resource and helped him find options and a key informational network. The primary issue to consider was financial. Paul was a long-time widower with grown children so he had no one financially dependent upon him. He had a modest house, part of which he could rent, but he was not sure that he wanted to continue the responsibilities of home ownership and being a landlord. He approached real estate people to find out how much he could get if he sold his home and a financial advisor who had expertise in investments and taxes to project how much money he would need and what he could expect to receive from investments as compared to home rental. He called the social security office to learn what benefits he could expect at what ages.

Paul did not want to leave the city where he had always lived, and his counselor nodded assent when he said that he thought it might be quite difficult to retire to the "sun belt," even though cheaper, because his network of friends was very important to him. As a single person, it would be very tough for him to begin anew in an unknown social environment. On the other hand, a trip to the west coast had long been one of his dreams for retirement, so he went to a travel agent to compare travel costs for plane, train, and motor tours.

Paul quickly realized that he would not have enough money to live as he would like if he did not obtain some kind of employment to supplement his retirement income. How could he find work that would also allow him some leisure time for travel and other enjoyable retirement activities? With his counselor, Paul began to brainstorm career change possibilities and to determine what lifestyle would be compatible for him at this stage of his life. He obtained information from the local university admissions office about what programs they had for retraining and career-change programs. He talked with the graduate dean about master's degree programs that could lead to administrative work in a church or hospital environment. Since he was not ready to make such a major commitment, he postponed that decision and decided to try some volunteer work, to see which experience fit with his talents and desires. He called the diocesan director of volunteer services to learn what opportunities were open that would meet his interests.

In the meantime, in order to supplement his income, Paul searched broadly for part-time employment options. He began to get a feel for the businesses in his area by scanning the yellow pages of his phone directory. Then the newspaper and word-of-mouth leads proved useful in generating many possibilities. He got help from his counselor and from the local library on ways to update his résumé, write cover letters, and prepare for interviews. He decided he would like to try work either in a fast-food restaurant or in a bookstore. He applied for both jobs and thought through what they would be like if he landed them. He decided he preferred the ambiance in the bookstore. He felt he would have more opportunity for quick advancement into management in the restaurant, and he imagined it could be "kind of fun" to sling hamburgers with the young people, but he realized that he might tire of the pace quite rapidly. Still, he did not let fixed ideas of status and respectability prevent him from acting and obtaining all the information possible before making his decisions. Three weeks later he received a call from the bookstore; they offered him an interview and were very interested in his background and motivation. He and the store manager negotiated a three-day work week with one month for unpaid vacation provided he did not take it during the summer when so many of the other employees were away.

When he decided to take the bookstore job, Paul knew that he was making a good choice. He had widely considered the possibilities open to him and had researched his options thoroughly. This choice allowed him some free time, some travel, and sufficient income to live modestly in the city where his friends would remain. He kept open the idea of going to graduate school by deciding to put aside some of his earnings for tuition while he explored church and hospital work on a volunteer basis. Paul knew he would be busy for the next few years but he was excited about trying out the new lifestyle. By postponing the sale of his home and remaining where he was, there was enough stability in his life to give him a sense of security as he ventured off in several exciting new directions. Emotionally he needed to grieve for a little while for the career and colleagues he was leaving; but the new doors he had opened quickly gave him renewed vitality, a sense of purpose and adventure in his life.

Like a hero, this businessman went out to fight the demons of dread, incompetence, and unemployment. He mastered the challenges and created the opportunities and outlook for a new life. His creative research was based on what psychologists call "divergent thinking." Recall the wide variety of resources Paul sought out. At the brainstorming stage, the counselor had advised him to consider everything, at least briefly, and not to discard ideas too rapidly. She encouraged him to seek the facts and try on all sorts of ideas for size. Brainstorming and divergent thinking are the mental aspects of action research. Then leg work and/or phone work is the vital key to keeping this process alive and realistic. The whole community is a potential source of informational input. And when anxiety arises, as it sometimes will, it is often helpful to ask, "Do I know enough yet?"

There comes a point in the creative process of problem-solving when you do have sufficient information on the table. If the number of options begins to feel a bit overwhelming, it is probably time to switch to the process known as "convergent thinking." At this point, you are ready to evaluate and narrow down your options. You will discard some that seem less satisfying and recognize that you may need additional information to clarify and further elaborate some of the possibilities that seem more appealing.

The process that Paul went through in career change is similar in many aspects to action research one might need for many different types of life problems. Whether it is a divorce, a career change, a medical problem, a geographic relocation, a problem with a child's behavior, or an educational opportunity, these basic steps are often similar. During the stage of divergent thinking, you need to obtain a whole array of information. To generate information from human sources, you will often need to locate the professionals or other helping people who can offer their assistance. These resources include people who are trained to provide medical, legal, emotional, educational, material, and/or financial information and help.

In addition to locating people in the community who can be of assistance, you also need information that will increase your own knowledge. There are many types of power a warrior may need, and knowledge is one of them. When you're feeling challenged, as if you are pitted against a strong foe, it is wise to remember: *knowledge is power.* You need knowledge to be empowered, in order to act effectively in your own behalf. With knowledge you obtain by active research, you can assume your appropriate role as a significant member of a team that you form to tackle the problem. Most problems require cooperative endeavor with input from at least several others in the community. None of us is self-sufficient and, as we work with others, the give and take of knowledge enriches each of us and facilitates effective problem-solving.

In this chapter, I will describe several aspects of action research in more detail. We will look first at locating and use of print media, along with the challenges of finding and using experts who can assist. Then I set forth in some detail the particular role of psychological consultation in relation to the varied problems that psychologists are trained to assess. You will want to be aware of the specific skills and training of any of the experts you call upon. A section on the available alternatives to standardized medicine will include a discussion of some of the possible advantages and dangers of such approaches. In the final section of this chapter, we will consider the attitudes and skills necessary to take charge of your life and to develop optimum, effective working relationships with helping professionals.

Finding and Using Resources

Taking the very first step to solve a problem is often the hardest. It requires overcoming inertia and getting into motion. Where do you begin to find the information you need? The first step almost invariably leads to numerous other possibilities. So the first step in divergent thinking is: BEGIN ANYWHERE. After you have internally considered your situation and know what your questions are, you can begin with either informational media or interpersonal resources.

Print Media. Your local library is a hub of information on almost any topic imaginable. In addition to books and journals, it has search capabilities that connect it to other institutions, including professional libraries. Universities, medical schools, and law schools, for example, have a vast network of print and microfiche articles that have been abstracted and categorized by careful researchers. Divergent thinking is made much easier by having such a wealth of knowledge so readily available.

Professional journals have one major drawback: they are usually written for people who have been initiated into the professional field and who, therefore, understand the jargon. For most lay people, the summary publications in ordinary English are much easier. The health field, in particular, has been showing considerable social responsibility by publishing newsletters and magazines for popular consumption. Subscription rates are generally quite moderate in cost. Some of the good health resources for the general population are listed in Appendix B, p. 197, and may be carried by your public library.

The phone directory is another hub of information that the careful researcher will need. The yellow pages provide an opportunity to scan the full range of services offered to the public. This approach may seem terribly simple, but how often do you use your phone without realizing "I am coping." And how often do you perhaps spin your wheels in a state of anxiety thinking, "There's nothing I can do!" Reaching out to discover the resources in the community *is* simple. Many of these resources can be as close and available as your fingertips and your telephone.

Networks. Most people, when they stop to think about it, have quite a wide array of resource people who can potentially be helpful in a variety of problem situations. One leads to another and soon you have quite a wealth of ideas and information. Suppose, like Betty, you need a lawyer to help with divorce procedures. When she had come through her gut-wrenching stage of indecision and had decided to go ahead with the divorce, Betty had talked to a close friend about finding a lawyer who was both strong and sensitive. The friend said she had implicit trust in one who did quite a bit of marital law. Betty was still feeling shaky about the whole idea of divorce, but began to feel a bit more secure when she heard her friend say this would be someone who would be tough enough to stand up to any pressure and fight for financial justice but still not one who would manipulate her into becoming "a barracuda." "That's just the combination I need," Betty thought. She had heard too many war stories about divorce fights and did not want the relationship with her soon-to-be-ex-husband to be made even worse by an insensitive lawyer who might try to "rev up the anger." Betty was smart; she knew just what she needed. More important, she knew what she didn't need! Betty was very sensitive to her own feelings and needs so she was able to choose a professional person with whom she could go forward in confidence.

Consulting the Experts. In many crisis situations in life, we need to turn to others who have particular expertise that we lack. When illness strikes, for example, many people have a family physician or an internist on whom they can rely. These doctors are often a good place to start when a particular type of problem arises. A referral network is operative among professionals who trust one another and who have seen evidence of competence and training. Often a brief phone call can lead to several referral names for whichever one of the multitude of specialties that you need. It is usually wise to get at least two names in case the first one is unavailable or doesn't work out for some reason.

But what happens when you find yourself face to face with a helping professional with whom you feel great discomfort? If you are receiving advice that you don't understand or if you doubt the wisdom of the advice given, it is wise, first of all, to let the professional know what it is you are thinking and feeling. Try to be to the point and brief in presenting your concerns, but be sure to let the other person in on whatever your reaction may be. This is a first and vital step in the all-important task of establishing good communications and what we call "rapport" with the helping person. Second, if the other person does not respond well or if you still feel some discomfort about the professional's advice, it is usually wise to get a second opinion. All responsible professionals should respect your right to full understanding and informed choice. Helping relationships are always built on mutual trust and, unless that rapport is present, the tasks are much more difficult for everyone concerned.

In crisis situations, there may be little time for the luxury of interviewing all the members of the professional team who will be your helpers. However, getting to know your helpers is an important aspect of cooperating. These are your allies in solving the more difficult problems you face. Choose wisely; these are people on whom you will depend.

Psychological Consultation

People usually seek out psychological assistance when they are aware of feeling unhappy, anxious, and stressed. Often they may not be at all sure about the real nature or extent of the problem. Just as physicians are trained to diagnose physical ailments, so also psychologists are specifically trained to diagnose and refer people for various kinds of treatment related to emotional distress.

There are "nodal points" in life where much change in individual or family life is occurring and stresses begin to take their toll. When it seems that one bad thing simply leads to the next and you feel you are in a downward spiral, then it is usually a good time to consider getting a psychological consultation. Cluster stresses commonly occur at the time of unemployment, divorce, the death of a family member, a diagnosis of a serious illness, a hospitalization, or the worsening of a chronic illness. Adolescence also puts added stress on many family members. Other times of peak emotional reaction include young people going off to college, a job change, geographic relocation, the well-known "midlife crisis," and retirement. Whenever a member is added or subtracted from the family system, there is needed adjustment for all concerned. These events are not always traumatic, but they may put added stress in a family system that's shaky for other reasons. Sometimes even much needed positive change can result in considerable upheaval both for the individual and for others who are close to him or her.

A couple came for psychological consultation saying they had separated and were considering divorce. Both were alcoholics in recovery. She had been in AA for three years, and he had stopped drinking one year before. Now, since they were both sober, life seemed better, but still they were having major problems getting along. This couple also had a little girl who had been diagnosed with a learning disability.

The psychologist doing the assessment recognized the significant, nodal events that had occurred in the past year. This couple had not yet been able to adjust to their daughter's learning disability and to the father's cessation of drinking. So much change had happened at once! Now, a year later, the mother was highly involved in the child's education and psychological state, and the father was still missing his drinking buddies and was staying out until all hours of the night. He was still visiting his old haunts even though he remained sober. He was not going to AA. The wife felt lonely, suspicious, overburdened, and fed up. She wanted a divorce.

Despite the alcoholism and learning disability, there were many strengths in this family. They had a great deal of love for one another, and both parents had already demonstrated their abilities to stop their destructive drinking behavior. The psychologist recommended family therapy for the couple and strongly urged the father to attend AA. There he would learn new ways to socialize and find understanding comrades. He would learn new patterns of behavior in the context of a caring community of people who could well understand his problems. AA would support rather than threaten his sobriety and his responsibility in the family.

A well-trained psychologist will do an initial assessment of the individual and family, questioning deeply into the situation as it is presented. Sometimes psychotherapy is indicated. In some cases, the psychologist will suggest additional testing to clarify the exact nature of the problem prior to making a referral. Neuropsychological testing, for example, can be performed in order to detect a learning disability, dementia, memory loss, or some other form of disturbance in thinking that might be the result of accident or illness. Other forms of psycho-diagnostic testing may be called for if there is a question of a differential diagnosis, to clarify emotional or physical causes of psychological distress. In some cases psychologists will refer clients for testing by other professionals, for example, for assessing visual acuity or hearing deficits or for career exploration.

Depression is one frequent presenting complaint that requires careful evaluation. The severity and nature of the symptoms of depression must be thoroughly assessed. In some cases, the person may be a potential suicide, and this is always taken most seriously. In other cases, even without somber preoccupation with thoughts of suicide, the person may be suffering from a clinical depression for which medication can be of tremendous help. In such cases, referral is made to a psychiatrist who can prescribe antidepressants or other medical treatment. Referrals are also made to psychiatrists when intense anxiety calls for tranquilizers or when thought disorder is present. The major mental illnesses almost invariably respond to the psychopharmacological treatments available from psychiatrists.

Choosing a Therapist. A very important aspect of the psychological consultation is the recommendation for psychotherapy. If therapy is needed, it is essential to determine which form of treatment would be most beneficial for the particular person or persons who are requesting help. The consulting psychologist should be familiar with a full range of the resource professionals in the community so that he or she can make the appropriate referrals. Each case is unique. Treatment should be individualized. There is no one form of therapy that is optimal for all cases. A description of a few of the more common forms of psychotherapy follows, along with examples of how different therapies would address the issues that a client presents.

Behavioral therapy is useful for specific problems that can benefit from focused, short-term treatment. Phobias, problems with assertiveness, and habit control (for example, with regard to smoking, insomnia, or weight) are among the conditions that respond most rapidly to behavioral treatment. In this kind of short-term treatment, other problems that may be mentioned by the client are bypassed by the behavioral therapist. The therapist will usually make a contract with you at the start of therapy and will focus attention on the specific, single problem at hand.

A middle-aged man requested behavioral help because he realized he was unable to be assertive with his aging mother. He found he would either get furious or capitulate and distance from her as rapidly as possible. He made a choice in favor of short-term treatment, saying that he did not want to get into the other related family difficulties. He was a successful businessman and clearly able to be assertive in most situations. Nonetheless, he felt intimidated by his mother, who had become quite cranky and complaining. He felt certain that he could cope better and reduce the stress in himself and other family members if he could simply focus and learn how to speak up to the old lady. The consulting psychologist referred him for behavioral treatment, as he requested.

Many times a lack of assertiveness or such a feeling of intimidation is merely a "tip of the iceberg." Other types of therapies might be even more beneficial in the situation just described.

Family therapy would view this case in a much broader context. Assessment would begin with questions about how the situation with the aging mother was affecting the whole family system. Are there other siblings? How are they reacting? Who is taking responsibility for the elderly woman's care? Are the daughters-in-law and the grandchildren being affected? The therapist might or might not want to call in some of the other family members to decide together what is best to do. The therapist would help the client(s) to view the historical perspective. How are the patterns of interaction now reflecting patterns of behavior that have been repeated in many similar ways over the years? Is the man habitually distant from others? Are there other areas of family dysfunction? What family values are at stake? In what way might the family members be co-dependent (that is, overly dependent on one another)? The therapist would be aiming to help the *whole family* to cope with the difficulties in relating to the aging matriarch. This situation would be viewed as a normative family process, and in therapy considerable learning would go on in relation to how the family interacts together across the generations. The aim would be to gain appreciation of the multigenerational transmission of family patterns and values. With this understanding, behavioral change would be more comprehensive, and changes would be appropriate to the needs both of the individuals and of the family as a functioning unit.

Individual dynamic psychotherapy is another form of therapy, one which is largely based on the views of Freud and his followers. In the case of the man who was unable to be assertive with his mother, dynamic therapists would explore the roots of the problem in the history of that relationship. Some dynamic therapists work in a short-term, focused manner. They would tend to explore the mother-son dynamics over the years and to look to the ways in which separation anxiety related to the mother's eventual death might be affecting the man and his current feelings about his mother. His inhibitions about talking honestly to his mother would tend to fall away as he gained greater insight. Those dynamic therapists who work at length (including psychoanalysts) would explore the relationship in greater depth and intensity. Issues related to the early mother-father-son triad would also undoubtedly come up. An examination of dreams and the client's relationship to the therapist would be aspects of treatment that would be found to relate to the client's central concern. The aim would be to help him work through his anxieties and hostility and lay them to rest.

Jungian psychotherapy or analysis might address some of the same concerns that the family systems and dynamic psychotherapy discussed with the man I described above. The primary focus would be in the internal world of the client, however. The therapist would ask him to recount his dreams, and together they would explore dream sequences extensively in order to gain greater understanding of his mother complex. Likely to surface would be a broad array of insights about his relations, not only to his mother but also to other women in his life. (As Jung discovered, men relate to women in archetypal ways. The image of the feminine within a man is what Jung called the Anima.) If this man should decide to continue in therapy for a year or perhaps longer, he would gradually come to a deeper appreciation of the mother-son bond as well as the conflicts that have been present over the years. He would see this relationship as an aspect of human life in its collective nature. And he would come to a significantly greater understanding of his own wholeness. The way his life has been and is affected by the female (Anima) people would be reflected both in his dreams and in his waking life. In Jungian therapy, he might also expect to achieve a deeper sense of his Self, of the purpose and the spiritual dimensions of his life.

There are numerous other therapies, but the important point is that the needs and desires of the individual client should be the guiding factors. The consulting psychologist should assess these needs and desires, comparing them with the process and outcome that are typically what we expect from the different types of therapy. A psychological consultation should provide very specific suggestions for what type of therapy would be most appropriate for the client with his or her unique presenting problem, personality, limitations, and resources.

Cost is one criterion that we must consider in a psychological consultation and referral for therapy. There are therapists with widely different training, and the costs of therapy vary accordingly. Counselors, psychiatrists, psychologists, and social workers may all have training to do psychotherapy, but there is a wide range of experience and background within each of these groups of mental health professionals.

It is not wise to go "bargain hunting" when searching for a therapist. Your whole personal well-being is at stake, and that is too precious to short change. On the other hand, it is not true that the most expensive practitioners give the best service. It is better to rely on a network of trusted professionals (including clergy) who will make referrals. Mental health clinics usually have competent staff so referrals can be to such a clinic if your funds are limited and you do not have medical insurance that covers psychotherapy. Usually only short-term treatment can be received at such centers, and sliding scale fees apply.

If in doubt about where to find a competent psychologist to serve as consultant, each state psychological association, usually located in the state capital, can provide the names of well-trained professionals and some information on their areas of specialty. Other sources to find listings of psychologists and their specialties are:

The Directory of the American
  Psychological Association
750 First Street, N.E.
Washington, DC 20002–4242

The National Register of Health Service
  Providers in Psychology
1730 Rhode Island Avenue, N.W., Suite 1200
Washington, DC 20036

Some university libraries and/or their counseling centers also have these listings.

Medical Societies and Self-Help Groups

When you are gathering information about a specific illness or injury, it is very helpful to obtain the brochures, reading lists, and advertisements to seminars given by many of the groups listed in Appendix B, p. 198. These medical societies and self-help groups comprise a vast network of helping services. They provide support and information to people in need. Many of the national organizations have state and even local chapters, so you can get nearby addresses and phone numbers from the national headquarters. You can find other sources of public information in health and mental health through your own state Department of Health, your local health association (probably listed in the yellow pages), and your local hospital. It is worthwhile being *persistent* in your efforts to gain the information you need. Your decisions will be wiser, your likelihood of health will be improved, and your coping with unavoidable conditions will be strengthened.

Alternative Medicines

In modern medical practice, overspecialization has led to an unfortunate trend toward depersonalization and a sense of fragmentation of patient care. The high costs and frequent use of invasive techniques (for example, chemotherapy as well as surgery) leave patients wondering if the technical miracles of modern medicine are really worth it. To combat this sense of fragmentation and depersonalization, the idea of "holistic healing" has reemerged from its ancient past. In the holistic perspective, the human organism is seen as one dynamic, self-healing energy system.

A comprehensive book by Richard Grossman entitled *The Other Medicines* explores a wide variety of the traditional folk methods that can be used side by side with modern medical and psychological techniques for the promotion of health and healing. Grossman describes such traditional methods as Hindu yogic therapy, Chinese medicine, and homeopathy. He lists numerous herbal preparations, along with exercises, and acupressure points for the relief of tension and pain. One example of this holistic wisdom is the growing appreciation that the energy, or fundamental life-force, that animates all living organisms has been recognized cross-culturally, throughout the ages. It seems that non-Western peoples were so attuned to nature and so acute in their observations of subtle energy differences that they learned to manipulate the energy even though they could not measure it. But now, with the emergence of new discoveries in quantum physics, scientists have come to acknowledge that all matter is energy and that even when matter appears static, actually it exists in a dynamic field. In fact, the *activity* of matter is the very essence of its being. The result is a modern-day rediscovery of ancient medical systems that have traditionally assumed the interrelatedness of matter and energy. Among these systems are the philosophical traditions of Taoism and Buddhism, each of which includes therapeutic methodologies. Hindu religion also has its related medical practices, and there are similar aspects in the more recent energic theories such as homeopathy. All these systems of thought embrace the notion of the universal vital force manifesting itself in all living things. This vital force is beyond measuring by microscopes or other instruments of conventional science. Nevertheless, it is a force that becomes evident in the vital efforts of the human body to heal itself and to become whole.

Dangers and Cautions. Let it be acknowledged loud and clear, however, that *not all* the supposed "healers," nor all the advertised "therapies" are, in fact, beneficial. There is a fairly widespread degree of quackery masquerading under the quaint-sounding names of New Age techniques for alternatives to medicine. There are three general methods you can use to research and evaluate information about alternative healing methods. First, be on the lookout and wary of quackery, being sure to ask about the training of the alleged healer and the theoretical assumptions on which the methods are based. Second, think clearly for yourself, questioning and evaluating everything you hear. Third, follow the guidelines you can find in comprehensive, authoritative, well-documented handbooks on holistic medicines. Finally, it is wise to be wary of anything that flies in the face of scientific evidence and to avoid all healers who purport to replace rather than augment the methods of modern medicine. Although modern physicians are clearly imperfect in many ways, they have, in fact, accumulated a vast amount of knowledge about the workings of the human body. There is still much that modern scientific medicine has not yet discovered but it is risky, even foolhardy, to attempt home-based remedies and a traditional or psychosomatic approach *instead* of needed medical treatment (for example, chemotherapy for cancer). The alternative methods can supplement but not replace the knowledge of medicine achieved through science. To take this caution lightly might actually endanger your life!

Taking Charge of Your Life

Because the variety of problem situations that may beset you in life is tremendous and because the potential resources seem to be almost infinite, what is called for is a process of tapping into your own creative problem-solving. We all have research skills and we all have creativity available if we can simply see the possibilities and imaginatively go after the solutions with perseverance and application of whatever energy is available.

In taking charge of your life, it is vital to recognize that you make your own decisions. This is not to deny that there are numerous situations where a certain degree of powerlessness is part of the problem. In fact, never will you be able to actualize your own desires completely and utterly. Many times you will need to surrender the desire to control and have everything your own way. Nonetheless, as long as your mind is in working order (or even partially so), you are the primary decision maker for your life. Whether you choose to be active or passive, whether you choose to take a leadership role or to be more docile and accepting of others' ways, you must always remember that you are making that choice. How you choose to act will have significant impact on the outcome of your coping efforts.

In order to cope effectively, your action research requires *self-awareness, assertiveness, and knowledge*. With self-awareness you are able to recognize, not only your thoughts and feelings, but also your needs, what you have to contribute to meeting those needs, and how you interact with others in the community who can be your helpers. With that ongoing sense of self-awareness as a guide, you are able to be appropriately assertive, that is, choosing your behavior so that it is neither underexpressive of your own needs and desires, nor overly aggressive. This balanced assertive approach will be effective in communicating with professionals and other helpers who will then become your valuable sources of support and knowledge. The knowledge that you will need depends on the nature of your specific problem. Generally, the more knowledge you are able to acquire, the more capacity you will have to work effectively in solving your problem situations.

Creating a Team. Whenever you interact with professionals or others in the community to solve a problem, you will need to keep in mind that solving problems is almost invariably a team effort. It is worthwhile to ponder this issue. How good a team do you have or can you create? Who are the strongest players? Who is the coach? The captain? Which team members play which roles? How much time are they willing and able to devote? What role do *you* play? Sensitive listening and effective communication are two key skills you will need to work with your team of helpers.

For example, when a child has a physical disability, learning disability, and/or an emotional disability, a team approach is needed. A team will form in order to help meet the varied and often extensive needs of that individual child. In school, the Pupil Personnel Team usually consists of the school social worker, a psychologist, a counselor, the principal, one or more teachers, and one or both parents. Emily was in the eighth grade and had cerebral palsy. That required her confinement to a wheelchair. She was bright enough so that special education classes were not necessary. The team goal was to keep her in the mainstream of the education process so that she could grow socially and emotionally as well as intellectually. The school social worker and Emily's mother worked closely together to identify Emily's needs and to call forth the resources that could be most helpful. (They became the unofficial co-captains of the team.) Both social worker and mother had, as their primary roles, the communication of Emily's needs to the other team members. The social worker talked with the school personnel and got periodic evaluations from the teachers as to how she was progressing academically and getting along with the other students. Emily's mother communicated with her physician, the physical therapist who worked with the child in the rehabilitation center, and of course with Emily herself and others in the family. The entire Pupil Personnel Team met together each semester to develop and then evaluate her Individualized Education Plan.

Toward the end of eighth grade, there was a dance for all the students in that grade. The team considered whether Emily should go to the dance. The counselor told the team that although Emily herself was a bit nervous, she wanted to go to the dance. She wanted to be with others in her class and experience, in her own way, what this social activity was like. After all, for eighth graders, dances are fun! Her mother felt overprotective, however, and she was afraid that Emily would end up feeling left out. The school principal then remembered an older student with cerebral palsy who was now at the high school. This student had managed to adjust quite nicely to social activities despite a disability similar to Emily's. The team decided to invite the older student to meet with Emily and her counselor so that they could discuss together how to cope. In a joint session, the two CP students talked openly and anticipated the left-out feelings and embarrassment that might arise by being disabled at a dance. The older student was encouraging and honestly enthusiastic about the dances. Emily began to feel more excitement. She really wanted to go. In the end, with support, understanding, and encouragement from many people, Emily went to the dance and had a lovely time. Her mother felt relieved when she learned that teachers had encouraged other students to talk with Emily, and they had done so cheerfully. Although Emily was "different" and always would be, she did not experience being left out from the dance and, in fact, learned that there are new ways to feel a sense of "belonging."

Regardless of the nature of the problem or the size of the team, it is wise if you view the interaction with helping professionals as a potentially cooperative effort. Often the patient or primary caretaking family member must act in the role of "principal communicator" among the professionals. Otherwise, the efforts of the helpers may be at counter-purposes.

When you are seeing more than one physician, for example, it is essential that the patient or caretaking family member communicate clearly so that each doctor knows what the other has said and done. *Do not assume that the professionals talk to one another!* In fact, they may be willing to do so but they will probably require your written permission and your request that they talk or share records with one another. (This is because the confidentiality laws and professional ethics that protect your privacy also block the informal communication channels.) More often than not, with the time binds that everyone is under, professionals unwittingly leave it to the patient or family member to be the connecting links. When you meet with your helpers, you will usually find it helpful to take notes and to briefly summarize the information you give so that each member of the "team" knows what is happening. Remember, when you involve experts who do not work in close proximity with one another, the sense of teamwork can only occur when you, as patient or primary caretaker, assume the role of creating and maintaining a cooperative team-like effort among the players. Communicate. Communicate. Communicate!

When Emotions Threaten Your Helping Relationship. When you as patient or client are involved in working with just one professional, the teamwork is usually called the "therapeutic alliance." Psychiatrists, psychologists, and social workers, in particular, are trained extensively in ways to facilitate rapport, that is, to develop and maintain an optimum alliance between you as patient and themselves as therapist. As Freud pointed out and is now well recognized, some of the feelings that any patient has toward a professional caretaker may actually be carry-overs from strong positive or negative feelings associated with the parents or other caretakers in childhood. This means that you may begin to feel toward your helper many of the same old feelings you felt with your parents. Sometimes these feelings are unrealistic and not really related to your present helping relationship. The only solution is to talk it out openly and to clarify your expectations. In addition to the expectations created by these emotional transferences, other feelings, dependency needs, and defenses from childhood may come into play. The more you are aware of the feelings and needs left over from your "inner child of the past," the more you can realistically discuss what your helper can or cannot provide.

When you have a significant physical illness, you will naturally feel somewhat helpless and dependent. You will tend to test a therapist's knowledge, techniques, and personal resources, hoping always that a miracle worker is by your side. Often these high expectations lead both you and your therapist to experience frustration. You somehow may feel it is hard to trust in a positive outcome. What both patient and therapist need is a sense of hope: hope that something can be done, some change can be made, that the problem can be relieved if not eliminated. When you have hope and when you as patient have some faith in the therapist as healer, then positive change has much greater likelihood of occurring.

Two threats to the therapeutic alliance may occur as a result of your own personality. One of these is an inability to verbalize the exact nature of the problem. Many patients have to struggle and learn to express both their feelings and the subtle nuances of their physical complaints. The other threat to the alliance is a tendency you may have to use denial as a defense. When in denial, a patient feels and says in effect, "There is no problem; I do not need your help." With medical illness in particular, denial may be a useful and needed defense against overwhelming feelings associated with traumatic injury or illness. But at some point, denial must be set aside so that both patient and therapist can work openly together, examining and mutually discussing the problems realistically.

Certain attitudes and behavior on the part of the therapist may also threaten your working alliance. When your doctor is too busy or otherwise unable to listen, the therapeutic alliance may never develop adequately, or it may be severely shaken even after some trust has been built. Not just psychotherapists, but all physicians and other helping professionals should develop good listening skills and a habit of taking their time to listen sufficiently well to the patient's or client's complaints. Unfortunately, this need for listening time is often *not* adequately met. Another problem in the personality of the professional that creates a threat to the alliance is an overly abstract, distanced, and objective viewpoint. Many of the helping professionals were trained in demanding, scientifically rigorous programs where there is no attention paid to emotional realities. As important as it is for professionals to understand and empathize with their client's emotional responses, this frequently does not happen.

Evaluating the Quality of Caregivers. If you should find yourself willy-nilly with a doctor who has no bedside manner, with an accountant who cannot tolerate your anxiety at income tax time, or a lawyer who is insensitive to your need to express grief or to move cautiously, *what can you do?* It is very clear that we all must rely on our care-givers. In time of crisis, you *may* need to simply plow ahead, making the best of the situation, proceeding along the path that has already been set. There may be little more that you can do. On one hand, you might wish to switch professionals in midstream. That might, in fact, be a desirable move. On the other hand, it may be more trouble than it is worth to break in someone new and begin again to establish the teamwork and therapeutic alliance.

Evaluating the quality of professional service is therefore best done at the very beginning, as part of the choice process. When you choose your professional helpers by personal references, you have the best source of network information available. If you make wise choices, ask questions, and get to know your helpers, the teamwork is readily es-tablished long before the crises occur. But clearly that is not always possible. Sometimes you must call in experts on an emergency basis. After the crisis has past, however, you always have another opportunity to reevaluate the people with whom you have been working. Wisdom comes only by learning through experience. Reflect and decide: next time, would you do it differently?

Evaluating the Process. Coping skills and coping resources are built gradually over time. Each individual has a wide array of skills and re-sources available. When you reflect on the process of coping, both as you are going through it and after you have passed each nodal cri-sis point, you come inevitably to an ever-greater wisdom and capacity to cope.

When you take action, becoming involved with helping profession-als, when you gain knowledge from the resources in the community, you are like a scientist in the ongoing research of life. As a warrior, you assertively approach the challenges you face. You use your information community creatively to solve problems. You act, you gather data, you reflect, and you learn. This is the essence of research, and this is the process of life.

8

Finding Your Own Way over the Waterfalls and Other Rocky Places

——— ❖ ———

THROUGHOUT THIS BOOK we have been reflecting on the coping process, considering the various options and analyzing the components of a broad coping model. We have looked at what works in various situations and for a wide variety of people. The parts are here before us, but how do we put it all together? For each of us, that is our own unique task in life. We must each build our autonomous way of living, defining who we are. Ernest Becker reflects on that unique meaning of life in his book *The Denial of Death:*

> When we are young we are often puzzled by the fact that each person we admire seems to have a different version of what life ought to be...how to live, and so on. If we are especially sensitive it seems more than puzzling, it is disheartening. What most people usually do is to follow one person's ideas and then another's, depending on who looms largest on one's horizon at the time....But as life goes on we get a perspective on this, and all these different versions of truth become a little pathetic. Each person thinks that he has the formula for triumphing over life's limitations and knows with authority what it means to be [human]....The thing seems perverse because each diametrically opposed view is put forth with the same maddening certainty; and authorities who are equally unimpeachable hold opposite views!

How can one cope with such vastly differing opinions on "the right way to live"? How can one manage in a pluralistic society, such as ours, to find a path of integrity? The one requirement, it seems to me, is to find one's own synthesis and to determine deep in one's own heart what is personally relevant, appropriate, and right. This requires nothing less than the discovery and the creation of one's own Self.

The search for Self has been described in many cultures, as a heroic journey, a therapeutic process, or a meditative goal. In this chapter, we will reflect on several approaches to the Self: listening to the *inner therapist*, reflections on *death* and the meaning of life, *"individuation"* as described by Carl Jung, and *silence* as deep nourishment for the psyche.

The Inner Therapist

A depressed man was contemplating suicide. He went to the hospital emergency room and heard they wanted to hospitalize him. He was terrified, feeling certain that if he entered the psychiatric ward he would never emerge again. While waiting in the ER for the doctor to arrive, he dozed and had a mini-dream in which his therapist appeared and said: "Now, Tom, that's enough of your negative thinking!" This dream marked the beginning of his healing. When the doctor arrived, Tom already felt considerably more optimistic. The "therapist within" had begun to take charge of directing his life. As it turned out, he went into the psychiatric unit overnight and was released, on a trial basis, the next day. He really began to work on his patterns of repetitive negative thoughts. The need to eliminate pessimism had emerged from within, and he found new meaning in the "power of positive thinking." The dream figure of his therapist represented a healing archetype constellated when he was most in need. He began to recognize and challenge the negative thoughts whenever they arose.

The archetypal healer or therapist within is often found in dreams of doctors, shamans, or therapists who represent an inner wisdom that can lead both to understanding the source of the problem and to measures that one can take to restore health, balance, and harmony. This inner healer is far more powerful and astute than any external therapist can ever hope to be. This fact has been known since the beginning of medical history. It was Hippocrates who said, "The natural healing force within each one of us is the greatest force in getting well." Many professionals and other healers recognize that the very best work that an external therapist can do is to facilitate a person's coming to know and respect the inner healer.

We are all multifaceted, that is, the psyche is constituted as a system of subpersonalities, each with its own feelings, attitudes, ways of thinking, vulnerabilities, and resources. What emerge in our dreams are pictorial images of these various aspects of the psyche. We can think of them as "archetypes" and "complexes" as the Jungians do, often personifying them in the language and imagery of ancient Greek mythology. For example, Asclepius is the ancient god of healing, and the Greek word *therapeia* refers to caring, supporting, holding, or carrying. Asclepius appears in many forms, male or female. For example, it is common to find dreams in which Asclepius appears as a doctor or therapist known to the individual. One such dream was of a woman in midlife crisis, searching for meaning:

> *I dreamed it was my birthday and I was chatting with a friend in her kitchen. Then she opened the door to the back yard where hundreds of people had gathered. In the center was Dr. P. and around him in concentric circles were all the people in my life! All the people I had touched and those who had touched me in large or small ways. All were significant. I was overwhelmed with a sense of gratitude. All I could say was: "All the people! Look at all the people!" I knew if I died at that moment, my life would be fulfilled.*

This woman recognized Dr. P. as the archetypal healer who pointed out that the meaning of her life was closely associated with relationship, whether brief or deep. Dr. P., the inner healer, was central in this dream, suggesting that something deep within — perhaps an insecurity or sense of meaninglessness — was being healed.

In ancient Greece, Asclepius was associated with the image of the snake, then thought to be a representative of healing. The caduceus symbol of modern medicine is a staff with two entwined snakes. Still today snake dreams may occur at the time of major life change, healing, and/or renewal. A woman in the midst of marital separation dreamed of a figure riding a horse around a circular path. There was jungle within the circle. The rider (who was unknown) had snakes arising up around his head.

Here Asclepius is depicted as the "healing warrior," and the chaos within, symbolized by the jungle, is bounded by the circular path. The horse and rider depict power and new energy. In real life, this dreamer felt the chaos of interpersonal stress all around her. She had been fearful about what her future would be and was intimidated by her husband. The dream brought her a sense of her own inner power, energy, and much-needed strength. The healer is an archetype that arises whenever physical or emotional healing is beginning. Recognizing this archetype brings joy and an influx of positive energy to facilitate and complete the healing process.

However she or he is imaged, when the inner therapist or healer gives advice, it is wise to listen and to try as faithfully as possible to follow the course of action suggested by the dream. If the advice seems not entirely clear, requesting additional information from the dream most often results in another dream that offers clarification, usually with a different dream imagery. So, too, with recurring dreams, it is especially wise to spend some time with the dream and its images. Meditation on the images, or simply holding them in mind during the daytime, will usually be helpful in unlocking the mystery. Once comprehended, the dream has done its job and the focus will move on to other things.

For all of us, pain and suffering are part of the flow of life. Giving up what we have loved, relinquishing ways of being that have been familiar and comfortable, and surrendering our too-limited images of ourselves is an ongoing, frequently painful process. It takes courage — even heroism — to step out consistently when new directions seem to call us onward.

When we look back, we often discover that the suffering itself is a call to transcendence. As Carol Pearson notes:

> Each time we become aware that we are suffering, it is a signal that we are ready to move on and make changes in our lives. Our task, then, is to explore the suffering, to be aware of it, to claim fully that we indeed are hurting.... [In] this way, suffering is a gift. It captures our attention and signals that it is time for us to move, to learn new behavior, to try new challenges.

Suffering, then, calls forth our need to change, our need to grow, to become more of who we can be. But suffering also calls forth the inner therapist, the wisdom-giver, the healer within. Pearson continues:

> Suffering is the leveler that reminds us of our common mortality, that none of us is exempt from the difficulties of human life. When suffering and despair come together, they provide us with the opportunity to affirm hope, love ourselves, and to say, against all odds, "And yet I will love, and yet I will hope!" It is then that we learn transcendence ... then that we know the beauty of oneness, of being part of the network of mortal connectedness.

When suffering is transcended by the inner healer, we come to know ourselves more fully; we come to recognize our place in the universe. Both inner and outer relationships are affected as we let go of the past and see more clearly in the present, more confident and trusting about the future. These are the gifts of meaning the inner therapist can bring. All that is required is openness, an exploratory courage and willingness to follow, step by step, when new directions emerge that are personally congruent.

The Future Is Death: How Can We Cope?

Whatever else we have in our individual futures, we all have in common one task ahead: that task is dying. Death is the great leveler, the great unifier. It is certainly that one aspect of life that all humanity shares.

Death is also, for many of us, a most terrifying fact. Probably the greatest challenges of life have to do with the way in which we cope with death. Death makes us anxious, deeply anxious. The inescapable reality of death can be denied, sometimes postponed, but never are the avoidance efforts successful. So let us look at that reality face to face. As we face the inevitability of death, we discover that death can be an advisor in life, a guide in all our decisions and the ultimate source of wisdom for setting priorities and determining one's personal meaning in life.

Death Anxiety. Death itself is a solitary task. Thanaphobia, or fear of death, is characterized by thoughts of the dying process, ceasing to be, and the unknown after death. Thanaphobia may be experienced, and to some degree resolved, early in life, but its ultimate resolution can only be in the abandonment and surrender to death itself. Most people do not want to die alone. Our personal, unique fear of death and separation is conditioned by other experiences of separation and loss early in life.

A cancer patient reported the following dream during a retreat when she was struggling to cope with the emotional effects of her disease:

I dreamed that I was in a factory, very cold and large. I was rummaging through lots of jumbled stuff, looking for something.

Then I was in a car. Someone was driving me to an unknown destination. We drove on and on. The outside scene became ever more desolate. We were going through what looked like a bombed out factory section. There was a dirt road being paved. It looked like a Russian work camp. All this was strange and alien. I never saw this place before. I worry: Why are we going on this road? It seems awfully barren and strange. Where am I being taken? Are we going to an even more desolate place?

The feeling of utter desolation expressed in this dream was a stark metaphor for the fear, loneliness, and despair this patient was feeling as she struggled to comprehend her cancer and what it would mean for her life. In similar circumstances, another woman dreamed of being isolated from friends, frightened because no one was home. She said, "I was afraid everyone was leaving me alone. I felt frantic and was trying to go with them. I was afraid they were abandoning me." In its stark reality, death *is* abandonment. It is total loss — saying goodbye to everyone and everything one has ever loved. Death is the ultimate deprivation, the final loss of self. It is abandonment of self by self. The fear of loss of self entails saying goodbye to everyone, never seeing the leaves turn orange again, no longer able to master the simplest task, cessation of brain waves with all their knowledge and experience. It is no wonder that those losses create such anxiety. To cope and master the internal stress of death anxiety, it is necessary to make peace with the losses one has suffered earlier in life before one can make peace with the final abandonment and loss that is death.

For family members and friends, relating to the dying person is a very significant aspect of the process of letting go. The dying person needs to maintain a balance between expressing precious love and intimacy and finding sufficient solitude for the necessary severance to take place.

In some families not all the members may be comfortable in supporting one another, so true equanimity and peaceful leave-taking may be difficult to achieve. Relatives may be personally defensive and fear that they too will be "pulled under" into depression and fear associated with death. Irrational fears arise when one confronts death, because reason cannot comprehend the enormity of it. Infinity is beyond imagination. As one eighty-year-old woman said, "I cannot imagine what forever means." Whenever one looks at death, the transitoriness of life is seen in fragile contrast.

Living with Dying: A Coping Paradigm. In most families, every member is intimately touched and impacted, either directly or indirectly, when a death occurs. Dying is a family affair. The type of death (whether violent or peaceful, due to a lengthy or brief illness), the age of the dying person, and the quality of relationships within the family will have significant impact on how the family members cope. A young person's death is often more difficult to accept than the death of an elderly person who has lived life fully. Death's effect may be sorrowful but felt to be a normal passage; on the other hand, it may have significant impact with many repercussions on the family's ongoing process and relationships with one another. Realignment of emotional forces following the loss of a family member may result in long-lasting change, either for better or for worse.

Let us look for a moment at the reality of dying in contrast to the stark imaginings. People tend to cope with dying the way they've always coped. Family patterns are similar to what they've always been — only more intense. Feelings are heightened and a mix of emotionality bubbles up in the family crucible. The emotional impact of death tends to follow the five stages identified by Elisabeth Kübler-Ross. In her powerful book *On Death and Dying,* she described the sequence of adjustment to impending death as denial and isolation, anger, bargaining, depression, and finally acceptance. These stages may recycle, however, and their impact is felt through the more habitual patterns of family interaction. Kübler-Ross found that all dying patients are "aware of the seriousness of their illness whether they are told or not." All need "to share some of their concerns, to lift the mask, to face reality, and to take care of vital matters while there is still time. They welcomed a breakthrough in their defense, they appreciated our willingness to talk with them about their impending death."

For those who fear abandonment even more than death itself, it is a vital gift to have an understanding person lend an ear from time to time. It seems that the call of Christ from the cross, "My God, my God, why hast thou forsaken me?" is the archetypal cry of the dying soul. If we are there to listen to that cry, to be present in that agony, the event of death is not so utterly alone. It is often not easy, but many families have found greater closeness and deeper intimacy than they have ever known before.

When there is someone dying, both children and parents have to cope with the fact that their family seems different from others. Any of the members may experience feelings of desolate solitude, power-lessness, or panic. Despite their own suffering, the adults usually try to stand firm for the sake of the family. They need to find inner con-solation and value in their will to persevere. They *have* the ability to raise their children despite the seemingly cruel blows of fate. Children also need reassurance about the family's ability to cope. They need to know, first of all, that their security will be maintained: the home will be there; they can still go to school; college options will still be avail-able. They may need, in addition, to learn gradually about the realistic limitations that may ensue.

Beyond the physical security, the children also need reassurance about their sense of belonging. Not only is the support of family mem-bers and extended family needed, but also the friendship network is most vital for communication of caring and support. An adolescent, in particular, may need to spend even more time with his or her friends in order to bolster the sense of belonging to the peer group and finding his or her place in the broader society. As Abraham Maslow has pointed out, self-esteem can be achieved and maintained only after physiolog-ical needs, security needs, and needs for belonging have been assured. When there is a death in the family, particularly the death of a par-ent, all these levels of security are threatened and adjustment requires support in each of these areas.

Either or both parents may try to cling to the children because of their longing for return to the happier days when the children were young or because of their own fear of loneliness and isolation. The "togetherness forces" in the family are strong at such times when the boundary of the family is broken and a key member is lost to the inevitability of death.

These tendencies toward togetherness and fusion eventually result in the counterforce of reactive distance, a moving apart as individu-als find their need for time alone is heightened. Distance, however, may create a sense of individual guilt when there is a death impending, and the rebound effect may be more pronounced. For these reasons, there tends to be more frequent, more intense patterns, switching pe-riodically between distance (which provides emotional space and an emotional "time out") and overcloseness (which provides a sense of love and comfort, albeit temporary). Such moments of respite, whether alone or together, seem to be psychologically necessary. Even though the system is in turmoil, the individuals must go on living, and their coping strategies may sometimes be unconsciously guided by their emotional needs of the moment.

A midlife family grieved at the time of the death of their father. At fifty-three he was too young to die. The teenage children felt cast adrift, insecure in a sea of uncertainty. The widow kept her mooring by writing in a journal, hastily recording the way their family coped with death:

> All week it's been family and community time. The overwhelming support of others is truly miraculous. I used to think wakes and funerals were inhuman. Now I see it as a community time to announce his death, and to receive support, to be strengthened so that we can go on. The message here is, "You are not alone." That's important. I need to know that. After the private alone-times, the one-to-one time for each of us to say goodbye to him, and the intimate family time, there comes the public time. I felt that my role then was to be the gracious recipient of all those offers of help. I felt like Jackie Kennedy was my role model. I wonder how many will be there for us in the months ahead?

During the ritual time, when friends and family gather, mutual support and interdependence are key elements. Each must give as well as receive. The difference between death becoming an uplifting event or a crisis for the family depends on how well the transition at the time of death is made. The potential for new growth is present. In time of passage, growth occurs when family members realize they are valued and that they are part of the continuity of time and history, part of a community with a heritage.

Bereavement groups can be a helpful way for family members to deal with their feelings and integrate the changes that are necessary in adjusting to a death. Furthermore, the support of professionals and other bereaved persons helps to take away the sting of loneliness. In one such group a man came to realize:

> Others have had it worse than we did. My wife had only a few months of illness and she was comforted by those blessed pain-killing drugs. She only had a few days in the hospital. I was by her side. It was a humane ending. I met others who had both parents dying at once! Some families have had four or five years of protracted deterioration. Some have had their hopes raised and then dashed. I think the worst is the rejection that happens in some families. Some people felt rejected

by their step-children, or their in-laws, or even (horror!) by their own
children! In the group we discovered, "It is the anger that alienates and
keeps you lonely." I learned that anger must be worked through! Talk
it out; don't let it rest and smolder.

In bereavement groups, families learn from one another. They learn
that not everyone is capable of expressing his or her feelings verbally. A
mother can relax, for example, when she realizes that her teenage son
does not want to talk but that he is working out his feelings alone when
he goes out every day to bounce his basketball and endlessly shoots
baskets.

Each person has his or her own unique way to grieve, and there is no
one right way to do it. For some, grieving is lengthy; for others it may be
brief and seemingly quite mild. Outsiders may not understand and may
be critical of quiet grief. Grief work is a personal, internal process. One
person may say simply, "I am suffering." Another may express anger at
the surviving parent. Each mourner is unique and can be encouraged
to do what feels natural to discharge feelings in nonhurtful ways.

Holidays are often difficult. Family rituals may be very needed. What
does a family do on Mother's Day when a mother has just died? Some
might want to visit the grave. Others might have a barbecue together.
The important thing is to decide together. Even though the family may
feel like a collection of isolated individuals, the vital message to convey
to one another is, "We're still a family."

A second or even third wave of distress may be felt by family members six months or more following a death. There may be unusual
conflicts among family members or illness in an individual. School fail-
ures, experimentation with drugs, heightened feelings of frustration,
excess sense of responsibility, burden, and loneliness, these are all common reactions and are considered by professionals to be within normal
limits. The problems should not be ignored, of course, but it is often
helpful to realize that they are grief-related and are likely to abate
if others respond calmly, without overreaction. Professional assistance
is often beneficial to help families weather the storms in the period
immediately following a death.

Like the dying person, each individual family member must confront
the reality of death, its personal meaning; and the way one copes with
that stark inner landscape is a very significant aspect of who one is.

Dreams and the Inner Wisdom for Coping with Death. Individuation, defined by Carl Jung, is the unique path that one travels to discover and create one's own wholeness. The end point, death, is a culmination of that journey, and dreams can be valuable guides in the last stages of the path.

One seventy-eight-year-old woman who was a cancer patient had this dream:

> I was visiting the Holy Land and got separated from my family and friends. I went into a church to pray for a while. When I came out, I stood on the steps of the church. In the distance, I saw my family. I didn't know whether to go and join them or to go back into the church alone. While I was waiting and trying to decide, my daughter waved at me. She seemed to be indicating that they were going on ahead. So I waved back: "Go on without me," and I went into the church alone.

This woman was getting ready to die. She had lived a vibrant life, full of energy and commitment to her family and the many friends in her middle European ethnic community. Church activities had always been an important part of her life but her style, until recently, had been quite extroverted. She was an organizer and a doer by nature. Now her dream called her to a more solitary type of passage. In the dream, as she goes into the church, she goes alone to face her God. In order to complete her life and find wholeness, this woman needed time alone and a solitary type of spirituality. Her family, on the other hand, needed to let her go. She told her dream to her daughter. Within six months, this woman's cancer had worsened and she died. She was at peace and the family had come to accept the inevitability of her death. They remained close up until the end. Each had privately taken time for the inner parting as well as the verbal "good bye." They had time to know and to say, "I love you. I will miss you."

Another dreamer was a sixty-five-year-old cancer patient:

> I was walking in the woods with a friend [someone who actually died of a heart attack five years before]. My friend was cordial and acted as a guide, but I was afraid and did not want to go.
>
> Then I was alone, walking up a mountain. A large black crow flew ahead and beckoned me onward. I trudged on up the mountain, past a restaurant, on up past the tree line. Still the black bird beckoned me onward. I reached the snow line. The bird was ahead, beckoning me onward. At the snow line, I stopped and refused to go further. Some-

how I knew that if I went past that line, it would be disaster. I returned
to the restaurant.
  Then I was walking in the woods with my deceased friend again.
The fear was gone now. My friend didn't speak, but he did put his arm
around me.

This dream was comforting to the dreamer in two ways: it relieved his anxiety about abandonment by providing a sense of needed
companionship to face eventual death, and it was encouraging in its
immediate prognosis. He gained a sense of death being a phenomenon
that was, for him, a "not yet" event. This man spoke of the many times
in his life when he had been to the brink, face-to-face with mortal
danger, only to return again and survive for another time. He had unfinished goals in his life and, as his dream predicted, he needed to say
"no" to the call of death and return to life for a while longer. He felt far
more confident after this dream: not only did he feel that his time was
"not yet," but he also felt his friend would serve as an inner companion
when the actual time for his death arrived.

Dreams may point to specific unfinished business to attend to before
death can come peacefully: a relationship that needs to be healed or a
project to complete or pass on to others. Spiritual goals often surface
in late-stage illness that require the patient to look more deeply into
the soul and reconcile his or her outlook on eternity or relationship
with God.

Death is a not uncommon theme in dreams at any age or state
of health, however. For example, a young woman who has recurrent
dreams of dead babies is struggling inwardly with her own tendency
to thwart each opportunity she has for new growth. We also find that
death and rebirth themes often arise in close proximity in dreams, sym-
bolizing life transitions where one must say farewell to an old way of
life before embarking on a new endeavor. In this sense, a dream of
death should *not* be taken as an omen or even as a necessarily frightening event. Rather, it is a sign of passage and perhaps a call to a new
outlook and new exploration of meaning in life.

For example, a newly retired, middle-aged man dreamed, quite
simply:

I met an unknown couple from India in native dress. The next day, the
man called me and said that someone had died and I needed to go to
the wake. He gave me directions how to go and to see the body.

This man had never been to India but had some knowledge of the customs there. Here is an archetypal dream, as referenced by the cross-cultural context. The dream calls him to view death. In India, death is clearly in evidence, both on the streets of the cities and in the sacred waters of the Ganges. What meaning could this dream have for a midlife American? As we discussed the dream, it became clear that the dreamer was in a quandary about what to do with the latter part of his life. In essence the dream seemed to say: Death is a reality you must consider. Your life will not go on forever. What is most meaningful for you? How would you spend your precious days if you knew, for a fact, that death would come soon?

Other dreams may be comforting for midlifers who face, perhaps for the first time, the inevitability of their own death, feeling the existential fear. One such dream occurred for a middle-age graduate student who was a nun, about to graduate and go on to teach in a new parish. She dreamed:

> I am preparing for a trip over the mountains. Everything is clear and brightly colored. The scene shifts to a nursing home. There are many old people there, infirm and in pain. Many seem to be our elderly sisters. I am afraid. Even the smells frighten me. I see an old white-haired woman in a wheelchair. She is all dressed in white with pale, almost transparent skin and blue eyes. I am touched because she is so frail and vulnerable. When I go up to her, she leans over and embraces me. After that, I have a real feeling of peace. I am ready to say goodbye and go on the trip. I know I must go.
>
> Then the scene shifts again and I am on the road. It is very hilly and I am accompanied by an unknown woman. I see twilight and shadows from the setting sun. I'm hesitant but I know I must follow this road. I start to drive down a very steep section when I awake.

Here is a woman reflecting on her future and facing the probability of eventual infirmity at the later stages of life. In working on this dream she came to recognize the archetypal journey of life and the wisdom of the old ones. The woman in white is a classical "Wise Old Woman" and the wisdom she gives has something to do with self-acceptance and recognition of the eventual journey into aging and infirmity. Yet the old woman affirms that state of aging in a nonverbal way. Her embrace makes it acceptable to be old. She seems to affirm the human condition. It is acceptable to be elderly and infirm; wisdom is present.

Death as an Advisor. If we image the specter of death as a great black bird hovering over our left shoulder, what can that mean for the way we approach life? Do we live in fear then? Or do we live in greater awareness? Do we cower in a corner, or do we look up and go forward to relish fully whatever time we have remaining? Stephen Levine, American Buddhist and author of *Who Dies?* has written of the profound meaning death can bring to whatever moments of life are remaining. His philosophy can be summed up by his saying, "Wholeness is not seen as the duration one has lived but rather the fullness with which one enters each complete moment."

How fully we enter into life is distinctly related to the quality of *awareness* we give to each moment. This fact was vividly brought home to me at a time of great loss in my own life. Separation, like dying, makes us acutely aware of what is most precious about what we are leaving. When I was leaving home, I had to say goodbye not only to my family and friends, but also to the house that had been my beloved home for many years and the entire town where I had grown up. There were many people and places I loved. I had not realized how much love I felt for all these things until I began the process of leave-taking. The "small death" of this separation made me open my eyes, my ears, and my heart far more than I ever had before. I saw more clearly the sun glistening on the little waves at the beach and the exquisite blazing color of the azaleas. I noticed more details like the little blue myrtle flowers tucked in among the leaves. I saw afresh the soft green of springtime leaves. I gazed on the houses and the people with new eyes. What beauty had been surrounding me and I had hardly noticed. I felt and expressed more of my appreciation. I could no longer take these people for granted. Each moment with a loved one was a treasure indeed. I could see the glint in a friend's eyes, could watch the gentle breeze wafting one's silken hair, could hear the timbre in another's voice. Why had I never before noticed that melodic resonance? The thoughts, the feelings, these were all treasures my friends and I could share.

Death and impending separations make us aware of how rapidly time is passing. Every day is precious. How little time we have to relish the beauty around us. Have you ever stopped to really watch a child (especially your own child or grandchild)? How quickly they grow up. This child, in this moment, is full of carefree delight. Can we, the more serious adults, really take the time to see and feel and be with the child at play? Watch his little dimpled knees as they bend and run and fall. Or see her little hands as she digs in the sand and splashes in the water. Listen to her shrieks of delight as little waves lap against her body. Or stop with the toddler who reaches down with mittened hands to scoop up and taste the new-fallen snow. That taste is such supreme freshness! Life through the eyes of childhood is a wonder. Through the eyes of one who is leaving, life has wonder and appreciation renewed. So along with death as an advisor, like a black bird over the left shoulder, we can image also a white bird hovering just over the right shoulder, singing a song of exuberant life and praise.

Death is thus our advisor because it increases awareness and intensifies our appreciation for the precious things of life. The counsel of death fulfills another function as well. With time limited, the important things come to the fore. Priorities come clear. There is no time for the insignificant. While at one level, there is a naive child in each of us expecting an unlimited lifetime, we are also aware at another level of the adult, realistic limitations of calendar time. We realize we make choices, and we are concerned about the swift passage of time. One way to help in any decision-making is to ask oneself, "If I had just a year to live, what would I do?" Given the resources presently available, how would I use them if I had only one year left? This question can be very productive in helping us to identify what truly matters to us. Life is too short and too precious to waste. Each choice we make, whether great or small, has impact on the quality of life both for ourselves and others. Death as an advisor keeps us on track. The eventuality of death reminds us of the precious moments we now have, and it guides our choices so that life itself will not be wasted.

Individuation

Individuation is the search for one's Self, one's unique personhood. In this quest, there are dangerous passages and threats to personal integrity, but despite the many pitfalls, the inner process inevitably seeks to make the best adjustment in given circumstances and to create the optimum development of the human personality. Perhaps, as the myth of the hero's quest would suggest, the sufferings and stresses of life all have a purpose in refining and strengthening the personality. This would be the viewpoint of those who believe there is a divine scheme of things.

We can think of the aim of our life's journey as finding that mythological "treasure beyond compare." That treasure is both something that perpetually lies ahead of us but, paradoxically, also lies within us and is fully and perfectly present all the time. We can conceive of the goal of life as wholeness, complete awareness, and acceptance of all the facets of the personality — weaknesses as well as strengths. This self-knowledge and acceptance of one's individual, unique identity leads to a sense of integrity. The Self, for Jung, is this coherent sense of personhood that is divinely inspired. He recognized that the process of psychospiritual growth is central for the individual and is depicted in dreams by images of centering. Jung, who studied many thousands of dreams of his patients in sequence, was convinced of the consistent development over time of the central symbol. This often was imaged as a mandala with pictorial emphasis on circles and squares and numerical emphasis on the number four and its multiples. These mandalas and other centered images, such as the tree of life, are found in dreams, myths, and art forms springing from the worldwide spiritual traditions. Jung recognized the imagery of centrality as a manifestation of a centering tendency existing within the psyche. In his book *Dreams* he wrote:

> The unconscious process moves spiral-wise round a centre gradually getting closer, while the characteristics of the centre grow more and more distinct. Or perhaps we could put it the other way round and say that the centre — itself virtually unknowable — acts like a magnet on the disparate materials and processes of the unconscious and gradually captures them as in a crystal lattice.... But if the process is allowed to take its course,... then the central symbol, constantly renewing itself, will steadily and consistently force its way through the apparent chaos of the personal psyche and its dramatic entanglements.... Indeed, it seems as if all the personal entanglements and dramatic changes of fortune that make up the intensity of life were nothing but hesitations, timid shrinkings, almost like petty complications and meticulous excuses for not facing the finality of this strange and uncanny process of crystallization.

In this way, we can think of the path of individuation as a progression similar to a cone where forward movement toward the vertex also spirals around, repeatedly returning to previous challenges. Each time we return, we find that we have grown a bit more, and we face that familiar old challenge with new insights, new strengths, and deeper understanding. Carol Pearson describes this spiraling process of growth: "Each stage has its own lesson to teach us, and we reencounter situations that throw us back to prior steps so that we may learn and relearn the lessons at new levels of intellectual and emotional complexity and subtlety."

This personal unfolding, like the blooming of a rose, is a miraculous process to witness and encounter. It is of paramount importance to trust the inner unfolding of your personality. This means trust both in yourself and in the natural power of the universe. Pearson writes, "Trusting yourself and your own process means believing that your task is to be fully yourself and that if you are, you will have everything you genuinely need for your soul's growth." The Self has been likened to an inner pilot or a gyroscope that keeps the personality upright and on course. Another image of the Self is that of an acorn, the small seed that "knows" infallibly the great tree that it is meant to be. Our unfolding is like the seed that grows into its ultimate intended form.

In Jung's view, that natural growth includes development of characteristics that have been traditionally assigned to both masculine and feminine interests. In normal maturation, by midlife an individual is capable of using a multitude of capacities that comprise the totality of one's personality. One can use both male and female qualities, for example, and acknowledge them as part of oneself. Traditionally masculine energies such as thrust into life and assertiveness can be fully developed and valued. So too can feminine energies such as the capacity for sensitivity and relatedness. Each of us, regardless of our biological gender, has capacities for both masculine and feminine energies and outlook on life. Wholeness entails being aware and comfortable with both the masculine and feminine within. That is the "union of opposites" that has been so persistently proclaimed, not only by Jungians but also by the mystics and spiritual writers in many cultures.

In Jung's view, *the unity of all pairs of opposites* is essential to the completion of the individuation process. In advanced old age, he wrote in his autobiography, *Memories, Dreams and Reflections:*

> I am astonished, disappointed, pleased with myself . . . distressed, depressed, rapturous. I am all these things at once, and cannot

add up the sum.... There is nothing I am quite sure about. I know only that I was born and exist, and it seems to me that I have been carried along. I exist on the foundation of something I do not know. In spite of all uncertainties, I feel a solidity underlying all existence and a continuity in my mode of being.

The world into which we are born is brutal and cruel, and at the same time of divine beauty.... Both are true: Life is — or has — meaning and meaninglessness.... The archetype of the old man who has seen enough is eternally true.... This is old age, and a limitation. Yet there is so much that fills me: plants, animals, clouds, day and night, and the eternal in man. The more uncertain I have felt about myself, the more there has grown up in me a feeling of kinship with all things.

One has a sense here that Jung himself was close to achieving his own goal of conscious awareness of the union of opposites. Good and evil are realities, both part of himself. So too is there a sense of simultaneous emptiness and fullness. Throughout his life, he was equally influenced by thinkers of the Orient and Occidental traditions. Here, at the end of Jung's life, the influence of the Orient with its emphasis on essential emptiness is combined with the mystical sense of fullness and rapture characteristic of Western spirituality.

For each of us, the goal is the same. Essentially, we seek the universal oneness, yet each must find his or her own unique path. We strive for the fullness of life yet we gradually surrender to the awareness of our personal poverty and limitations. In the emptying that occurs as we reach the threshold of death, we have the final opportunity to find a deeper awareness and appreciation for all of life just as it is.

Silence

Full awareness of life as we are living it requires that we be sensitive and fully present in the moment. To stay with the moment-to-moment interactions is a mental discipline, not onerous but joyful. We can put aside memory and desire in order to live life fully in the *now*. This Zen-like state is not reserved for monks of esoteric religious orders but is available to ordinary people who wish to heighten their awareness in order to live more vibrantly. In the inner place of silence lies the source of healing, renewal, and inspiration. Our post-modern world with its busyness and stress leaves many people starving for the nourishment of silence. To find time to put aside words and quiet the thoughts is to find an inner retreat that brings nourishment and peace.

In one of the coping workshops I offer to the public, the final session was devoted to integrating the six coping styles and determining which would be most effective in each person's own life. Two seemingly very different individuals found themselves at a point of agreement: A workman, a father of five and grandfather of thirteen, was kind and generous but felt guilty when his children visited; he wanted to escape the family and find refuge in his workshop. "Why don't I want to be with my grandchildren?" he asked himself. There must be something wrong; maybe I don't love them enough." A young mother of three was also a lawyer with a part-time practice. "I love my husband and children," she said, "but I need to get away from them. Sometimes I get so antsy with the children around that I just am dying for some peace and quiet!"

Both these people were in significant need of alone-time. One should not feel guilty for having that need. Especially for introverts, ample time for silence is vital. Extroverts, too, need at least some time alone, a balance of time to quiet the thoughts and silence the words. When life is busy, finding the time — making the time — for a brief respite of silence may be one of the most effective methods of coping ever devised. Often what we most need is to give ourselves permission for a brief "time out."

In silence, you feel the nonverbal presence of life around you, the softness surrounding and comforting you. In silence, attune to the rhythm of nature and attune to your own rhythm:

> The rhythm of waves by the shore...
> of birdsong in the trees above...
> The rhythm of quiet work...
> of breath...
> of heartbeat...
> The rhythm of sleep, and rest...
> and nourishment...
> Rhythms of giving and receiving from the
> natural world around you.

In silence, you can listen to the quiet breezes blowing; listen to country noises or city noises; listen to the support world around you, the humming of the refrigerator, the ticking clock, the distant siren of the ambulance on its way in a mission of mercy. In silence, you have space to stop the busyness, to affirm gratitude, to find the inner central place of peace.

Many years ago, when I was first learning to meditate, I experimented with numerous ways of going into the inner place of silence. It was hard to find time in those days. The children were small, and there were constant demands on my time and attention. Nonetheless, I resolved to take some time for silence and meditation each day. (Sometimes it was early morning, or late at night, or during the children's nap time or when they were out and safely at play.) All the meditative practices I explored helped to reduce anxiety and restore a cheerful mood. One meditation I read about had a particularly profound effect when I tried it. As directed, I calmed my mind and then looked into a mirror and asked, "Who are you?" The answer that slowly arose came back to me from a deep meditative place:

> I am who you want me to be.
> You are who I want you to be.

Such simple words but such a profound implication. I sensed that I had received a glimpse of the "Zen mirror"; that the anonymous presence that we call God is in essence all of our highest ideals, all of our most cherished desires. And simultaneously, there was the knowing that at heart, in my truest inner Self, I reflect the desire of that Being, that Presence. The divine within and the Divine without are simultaneously reflected in that mutual desire, that present acceptance, and ultimate perfection.

Coping with life with all its problems, coping with death and its ultimate challenge, coping with the frequently painful, transformative process, this is the task put before us. This is the challenge we live.

When we look around us, we see all manner of people living their own particular life tasks: life and work all about us. The challenges abound. Moments of ease seldom last for long. But a reverence for life is cultivated in the silence. Birth, growth, plateau, decay, and death, all are one. In the cycle of life, we can reach beyond merely coping. We can meet the difficulties and master the challenges. At each stage, life offers us opportunities for growth. Whether body, mind, or spirit, there is always an upward thrust. In silence, we discover the Spirit of life ever renewed.

Being and becoming intertwine. Acceptance of life as it is allows us all freedom to become ourselves. The yearning for perfection is mirrored by the loving acknowledgement that life is rich and full, just as it is.

Like the stream that passes by, life is sometimes rapid, sometimes gentle. We too must find our way past tree stumps and over waterfalls. We too must respond to rocky places and limitations. Cascading downward, dynamic, ever flowing onward, we too descend to the sea that envelops our entire being. We too seek our place amid the greater whole.

Appendix A

Exercises

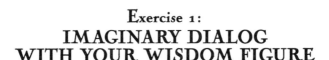

Exercise 1:
IMAGINARY DIALOG
WITH YOUR WISDOM FIGURE

For this and other body/mind/body/spirit exercises, it usually works best to read through the directions first and then begin the practice. If you choose to repeat it and enter the experience more deeply, you might want to make a tape of the instructions and play it back, freeing yourself to participate fully in the experience. For this exercise, you may choose any wisdom figure, perhaps Jesus, Buddha, the Divine Mother, or any wise person you know. Often it is most effective to let the figure emerge spontaneously and then see who it is. Be sure to leave plenty of time in the pauses, and begin with gentle, leisurely relaxation.

•

Sit comfortably in a position in which your arms and legs are supported and your back is straight. Breath deeply several times.... Notice your breathing.... Let your breathing become natural, rhythmic....

When your eyes become heavy, they will want to close. You will want to let your eyes close ... let your eyes close....

In your mind's eye, you see ahead of you a lovely meadow. Notice the sunlight on the grass ... the flowers.... Notice the colors.... Smell the delightful aromas of the meadow.... Is that honeysuckle? ... Feel the gentle breeze and notice how the grasses blow....

On the left border of the meadow you notice some trees.... There under the dappled shade you notice a bench.... The place looks refreshing.... You want to go there ... let yourself go there.

How comfortable it looks ... the bench feels comfortable as you sit, as you relax in the shade, in the dappled sunlight.... As you look up at the leaves overhead, you see the patterns of light and shade ... gently blowing leaves ... light and shade ... gently blowing ... very comfortable....

As you sit in this relaxed place, you notice a person coming toward you. . . . As this person is getting closer, you begin to see who it is. . . . Invite this person to sit with you . . . to talk with you. . . .

You may talk about how you feel right now. . . . And talk about the difficulties in your life that concern you right now. . . . And tell this person how you feel about him or her. . . . Now rest in the silence of this presence for a while. . . . And let this person tell you how he or she feels about you. . . .

After you have finished your conversation, you stand up and say goodbye to one another. Is there a final message to exchange? . . . A final gesture? . . . It is now time to come back through the meadow. . . . Come back to this room. . . . As you return, you continue to feel relaxed and you are getting more and more alert . . . more alert with each breath that you take. . . .

Count now from three backward to one. When you reach the number one, it will be time to open your eyes, completely refreshed, and to return to normal waking consciousness.

3. Breath in . . .

2. Exhale . . .

1. *Open your eyes*, refreshed, awake, and alert!

Exercise 2:
BODY AWARENESS

Find a comfortable position, perhaps lying on your back with your knees up so that your feet rest flat. Close your eyes and become aware of your body. . . . As you focus your awareness on your body and your physical sensations, notice first your breathing. Focus your attention on your breathing. . . . You may notice that thoughts or images come to mind. Instead of trying to stop your thoughts and imaginings, just focus your attention instead on your breathing. . . . Whenever you find your mind has wandered, just refocus your attention on the physical sensations of breathing. . . .

There's no need to struggle . . . just notice when you become preoccupied, and then return your attention to your breathing. . . . Try breathing deeply so that the air fills and lifts your abdomen. . . . Try in-haling through your nostrils and then exhaling through your lips. . . . As you inhale and as you exhale, feel the temperature of the air crossing your nasal passages and lips. . . .

Now let your awareness drift across your body. Notice your physical sensations. Notice any movement, tension, or discomfort. . . . As you notice these sensations, realize that you are doing the pushing, tens-ing, or holding. . . . What happens when you exaggerate a movement? If you feel a little tension in your neck, tense it more. Be aware of your responsibility and your control over that tension. Now let it go. . . .

See if you can get more comfortable by changing your position slightly. . . . Now in a comfortable way, just run your awareness over your body several times. Notice the feel of your head. . . . the sensa-tion around your eyes . . . your cheeks . . . your neck. Feel the texture of the clothes resting on your shoulders . . . or your chest. . . . Notice your right upper arm, lower arm, hand. . . . Now your left arm, lower arm, hand. . . . Feel the weight of your body resting on your buttocks. . . . Notice your right thigh, calf, foot. . . . Feel your left thigh, calf, foot. Do not dwell on any one body part for more than a few seconds.

Now, return your awareness to your head again. Notice the sensa-tion in your head . . . shoulders . . . right arm . . . right hand . . . left arm . . . left hand . . . chest . . . buttocks . . . thighs . . . calves . . . feet.

Now again sweep your awareness from head . . . to shoulders . . . arms . . . torso . . . right leg . . . left leg . . . right foot . . . left foot.

Now let your awareness freely drift again. Are there any parts of your body that you want to attend to for a moment? Breathe naturally and notice how that feels. Notice any residual tension or any movement. Can you feel your heartbeat pulsing through your body?

When you are ready, open your eyes. Notice how the light affects your experience of your body. As you stand up again, experience the movement and the kinesthetic balance that you create. Stay with that body awareness as long as you can. Come back to it during the day.

Exercise 3:
THREE-PART BREATHING

It is best to learn this exercise while lying flat on your back with your knees raised and feet flat on the floor or bed. Later, it can be done in any position.

- Begin with abdominal breathing. Inhale through your nostrils, letting the air flow into your abdomen, with your belly rising as in the previous exercise. Exhale through your mouth, being sure to expel all the air and flatten your abdomen.

- Then place a hand on your chest at the level of the rib cage. Inhale into your abdomen as before, feeling your belly rise. Next, continue the inhalation, feeling your rib cage expand (moving outward) as you bring the air into your chest. Exhale through your mouth, first emptying your abdomen (flattening your belly) and then emptying your chest cavity. Exhale completely.

- With your hand still on your chest, add the third part of the breath. Inhale through your nostrils, first filling your abdomen (belly up), then filling your chest (rib cage out). Complete the inhalation by allowing the air right up through your torso, feeling your shoulders rise. Exhale through your mouth in the same order, first flattening your belly, then compressing your chest, finally lowering your shoulders. Be sure to exhale completely, squeezing out the last bit of air.

Exercise 4:
SALUTE TO THE SUN

Each breath should be the three-part breath described in the previous exercise.

- Stand erect with your palms together at chest height in a "prayerful" pose.

- Inhale as you raise both arms overhead, hands apart at shoulder width, arching your spine and arms backward.

- Exhale as you bend forward, touching your hands to the ground before you, keeping your legs as straight as possible.

- Inhale as you extend the right leg backward, arching your head and spine upward, looking up toward the sky.

- Exhale as you extend your left leg backward, parallel to the other leg and then drop on both your knees to the ground. At the end of the exhalation, let your body down to the floor.

- Reverse the process, inhaling as you raise your right leg, leaving your left leg extended behind and arching your back with head upward.

- Exhale as you bring your back foot forward to meet the right one, keeping hands on the ground and legs as straight as possible.

- Inhale as you raise your torso with arms overhead, arching backward.

- Exhale as you lower your arms to the chest-high position with palms together.

- Repeat, using your left leg to lead. Repeat two times alternating on each leg.

—————— ❖ ——————

Exercise 5:
JACOBSONIAN METHOD OF RELAXATION

- Sit or lie down in a comfortable position with your legs and arms uncrossed. Close your eyes and begin with a few deep breaths. ...Now with your right hand, make a fist. Feel the tension as it extends up your right arm.... Now release and relax, letting all the tension go. Notice the difference and how you make that change happen....

- Now again make a fist and bring it up to your shoulder, so that you "make a muscle, like Popeye." Feel the tension in your arm and shoulder. Then relax, let the arm drop and notice the difference....

- Repeat with left fist....

- Left arm....

- Now scowl and feel the way your forehead, face, and scalp tense up. Release and relax... notice the difference.

- Clench your jaw and feel the tension in your cheeks, chin, and neck. Then release, relax, and notice how to do that....

- Tighten your shoulder blades and upper chest. Feel the tension and then release....

- Tighten your buttocks and abdomen. Feel the large muscles. Feel how tight they can be.... Now release; relax. Notice the difference. Feel the comfort.

- Now extend your right leg forward with your foot pointing up toward the ceiling. Tense all the muscles in your calf and thigh. Lock the knee and feel the tightness. Then let go; let the leg drop. Release all the tension and feel the difference.

- Repeat with the left leg, feeling the relaxation that follows....

- You can repeat this exercise, tensing and releasing each body part progressively before moving on. Complete the exercise with a few deep breaths. Allow yourself a few extra minutes to sit, feeling relaxed, before resuming your normal activities.

Appendix B

Resources

HEALTH NEWSLETTERS

Advances: The Journal of Mind-Body Health
Published quarterly by Fetzer Institute
9292 West KL Avenue
Kalamazoo, MI 49009-9398

The Ardell Wellness Report
Planning for Wellness
Campus Wellness Center
University of Central Florida
Orlando, FL 32816
(407) 823-5841

Harvard Medical School Health Letter
Published monthly by the Department of Continuing Education
79 Garden Street
Cambridge, MA 02138
(617) 432–1485

Health Action for a Productive Life
410 East Water Street
Charlottesville, VA 22901

Health Resources
Published monthly by Kelly Communications
410 East Water Street
Charlottesville, VA 22901
(804) 296–5676

Prevention
Published monthly by Rodale Press
33 East Minor Street
Emmaus, PA 18098
(215) 967–5171

University of California, Berkeley Wellness Letter
Published monthly by Health Letter Associates
Subscription information: P.O. Box 10922
Des Moines, IA 50340

REFERRAL SOURCES

AL-ANON Family Groups Headquarters, Inc.
1372 Broadway
New York, NY 10018–6106
(212) 302–7240
Mailing address:
  P.O. Box 862
  Midtown Station
  New York, NY 10018–0862

Alcoholics Anonymous
World Services, Inc.
468 Park Avenue South
New York, NY 10016
(212) 870-3400
Mailing address:
  Box 459
  Grand Central Station
  New York, NY 10163

American Academy of Ophthalmology
655 Beach St.
San Francisco, CA 94109
(415) 561-8500

American Cancer Society
Cancer Information Service
(800) 4–CANCER

American Heart Association
National Center
7320 Greenville Avenue
Dallas, TX 75231
(214) 987-1058

American Self-Help Clearinghouse
St. Clare's Riverside
Medical Center
Denville, NJ 07834
(201) 625–7101

Incest Survivor Information Exchange
P.O. Box 3399
New Haven, CT 06515

Lupus Foundation of America
4 Research Place, Suite 180
Rockville, MD 20850-3226
(301) 670-9292

Narcolepsy Network
P.O. Box 1365
FDR Station
New York, NY 10150

National Alliance for the Mentally Ill
2101 Wilson Boulevard, Suite 302
Arlington, VA 22201
(703) 524-7600 or (800) 950-6264

National Arthritis Foundation
1314 Spring Street Northwest
Atlanta, GA 30309
(404) 872-7100

National Head Injury Foundation
1776 Massachusetts Avenue, N.W., Suite 100
Washington, DC 20036
(202) 296–6443

National Multiple Sclerosis Society
Executive Headquarters
733 Third Avenue, 6th Floor
New York, NY 10017
(212) 986-3240

National Society to Prevent Blindness and Its Affiliates
160 East 56th Street
New York, NY 10022
(212) 980-2020

U.S. Department of Health & Human Services
9000 Rockville Pike
Bethesda, MD 20892

READING LIST

Achterberg, Jeanne. *Imagery in Healing: Shamanism and Modern Medicine.* Boston: New Science Library/Shambhala, 1985.

Bauman, Edward, Armand I. Brint, Lorin Piper, and Pamela A. Wright, eds. *The Holistic Health Handbook: A Tool for Attaining Wholeness of Body, Mind, and Spirit.* Compiled by the Berkeley Holistic Health Center. Berkeley, Calif. AND/OR Press, 1978.

Becker, Ernest. *The Denial of Death.* New York: Macmillan, 1973.

Benson, Herbert. *The Relaxation Response.* New York: Morrow, 1975.

Bianchi, Eugene. *Aging as a Spiritual Journey.* New York: Crossroad, 1987.

Bolen, Jean Shinoda. *The Tao of Psychology: Synchronicity and the Self.* San Francisco: Harper & Row, 1979.

Borysenko, Joan, with Larry Rothstein. *Minding the Body, Mending the Mind.* Reading, Mass.: Addison-Wesley, 1987.

Campbell, Joseph. *The Hero with a Thousand Faces*. Princeton, N.J.: Bollingen, 1973.

Carlson, Richard, and Benjamin Shield, eds. *Healers on Healing*. Los Angeles: Jeremy P. Tarcher, 1989.

Carrington, Patricia. *Freedom in Meditation*. Garden City, N.Y.: Doubleday Anchor, 1978.

De Mello, Anthony. *Sadhana: A Way to God: Christian Exercises in Eastern Form*. Garden City, N.Y.: Doubleday Image, 1984.

Frank, Jerome. *Persuasion and Healing*. New York: Schocken, 1973.

Gendlin, Eugene T. *Let Your Body Interpret Your Dreams*. Wilmette, Ill.: Chiron, 1986.

Gibran, Kahlil. *The Prophet*. New York: Knopf, 1973.

Grossman, Richard. *The Other Medicines: An Invitation to Understanding and Using Them for Health and Healing*. Garden City, N.Y.: Doubleday, 1985.

Guerin, Philip J., ed. *Family Therapy: Theory and Practice*. New York: Gardner Press, 1976.

Hall, James. *Jungian Dream Interpretation: A Handbook of Theory and Practice*. Toronto: Inner City Books, 1983.

Halligan, Fredrica R., and John J. Shea, eds. *The Fires of Desire: Erotic Energies and the Spiritual Quest*. New York: Crossroad, 1992.

Hillman, James. *A Blue Fire*. New York: Harper & Row, 1989.

Jung, Carl G. *The Development of Personality*. Collected Works 17. Princeton, N.J.: Bollingen, 1954.

———. *Memories, Dreams and Reflections*. New York: Pantheon, 1973.

———. *Dreams*. Princeton, N.J.: Bollingen, 1974.

Kelsey, Morton T. *The Other Side of Silence: A Guide to Christian Meditation*. New York: Paulist Press, 1976.

Kübler-Ross, Elisabeth. *On Death and Dying*. New York: Macmillan, 1969.

Kutash, I. L., L. B. Schlesinger, and Assoc., eds. *Handbook on Stress and Anxiety*. Washington: Jossey-Bass, 1980.

Lazarus, Richard S., and Susan Folkman. *Stress, Appraisal and Coping*. New York: Springer, 1984.

Levine, Stephen. *Who Dies? An Investigation of Conscious Living and Conscious Dying*. New York: Anchor, 1973.

Pearson, Carol. *The Hero Within: Six Archetypes We Live By*. San Francisco: Harper & Row, 1986.

Peck, Scott. *The Different Drum: Community-Making and Peace*. New York: Simon & Schuster, 1987.

Sanford, John. *Dreams: God's Forgotten Language*. New York: Harper & Row, 1989.

Segal, Julius. *Winning Life's Toughest Battles.* New York: McGraw Hill, 1986.

Siegel, Bernie S. *Love, Medicine and Miracles: Lessons Learned about Self-Healing from a Surgeon's Experience with Exceptional Patients.* New York: Harper & Row, 1986.

Ulanov, Ann B., and Barry Ulanov. *Primary Speech: A Psychology of Prayer.* Atlanta: John Knox, 1982.

Ullman, Montague, and Nan Zimmerman. *Working with Dreams: Self-Understanding, Problem-Solving and Enriched Creativity through Dream Appreciation.* Los Angeles: Jeremy P. Tarcher, 1979.

Underhill, Evelyn. *Mysticism: A Study in the Nature and Development of Man's Spiritual Consciousness.* London: Methuen, 1911.

Valliant, George E. *Adaptation to Life.* Boston: Little, Brown, 1977.

Watkins, Mary. *Waking Dreams.* Dallas: Spring, 1984.

Whitmont, Edward C. *The Symbolic Quest: Basic Concepts of Analytical Psychology.* Princeton, N.J.: Princeton University Press, 1969.

Whitmont, Edward C., and Silvia B. Perera. *Dreams: A Portal to the Source.* New York: Routledge, 1989.